MICKEY HART
AND FREDRIC LIEBERMAN
WITH D.A. SONNEBORN

PLANET DRUM

A CELEBRATION OF PERCUSSION AND RHYTHM

HarperSanFrancisco
A Division of HarperCollinsPublishers

PLANET DRUM

A Celebration of Percussion and Rhythm

Copyright © 1991 by Mickey Hart. All rights reserved. Printed in
the United States of America. No part of this book may be
used or reproduced in any manner whatsoever without
written permission except in the case of brief quotations embodied in
critical articles and reviews. For information address
HarperCollins*Publishers,* 10 East 53rd Street, New York, NY 10022.

DESIGNED AND PRODUCED AT TRIAD
BY HOWARD JACOBSEN

ASSOCIATE ART DIRECTION: CAROL HOOVER

FIRST EDITION

LIBRARY OF CONGRESS
CATALOGING-IN-PUBLICATION DATA
Hart, Mickey.
Planet Drum : a celebration of percussion and rhythm / Mickey Hart
and Fredric Lieberman, with D. A. Sonneborn. — 1st ed.
p. cm.
Includes bibliographical references, discography, and index.
ISBN 0-06-250414-2 (cloth) — ISBN 0-06-250397-9 (pbk.)
1. Drum. 2. Music, Origin of. 3. Musical meter and rhythm.
4. Percussion instruments. 5. Percussion music — History and criticism.
6. Folk music — History and criticism.
I. Lieberman, Fredric. II. Sonneborn, D. A. III. Title.
ML1035.H37 1991 786.9—dc20 90-56463 CIP MN

**GRATEFUL ACKNOWLEDGMENT FOR PERMISSION TO QUOTE FROM
THE FOLLOWING COPYRIGHTED SOURCES**
The Art of Noises: A Futurist Manifesto, by Luigi Russolo, translated by
Robert Filliou. Courtesy of Richard C. Higgins. *The Sun Book,*
Jelaluddin Rumi, translated by Coleman Barks. Reprinted by permission of
Maypop Books. "The Vision of Tailfeather Woman" as told by
William Bineshi Baker, in Thomas Vennum, Jr., *The Ojibwa Dance Drum: Its History
and Construction.* Reprinted by permission of Smithsonian Institution Press.

SEVERAL STORIES IN *PLANET DRUM* HAVE BEEN ADAPTED FROM PUBLISHED WORKS
"How Universe, the Supreme Being, Makes Rain" and "Morgon-Kara" are based on
the versions in Joseph Campbell. *Historical Atlas of World Mythology, Vol. 1: The
Way of the Animal Powers* (New York: Harper & Row, 1983). "Bullroarer Comes to
the People" is based on an account received from an anonymous
source. "The Origin of the Wooden Drum" is based on Hugo Zemp. *Musique
Dan: La Musique dans la pensée et la vie sociale d'une societé africain* (Paris: Mouton & Co.,
and École Pratique des Hautes Études, 1971). "The Human Drum" is
based on Fernando Montesinos. *Memorias antiguas historiales del Peru,* translated and
edited by Philip Ainsworth Means (London: Hakluyt Society, 1920).
"Tsar-Kolokol" is based on Edward V. Williams. *Bells of Russia: History and
Technology* (Princeton, NJ: Princeton University Press, 1985). "The
Soul of the Great Bell" is based on Lafcadio Hearn. *Some Chinese Ghosts* (New
York: Modern Library, 1927). First published: Roberts Brothers, 1887.

91 92 93 94 95 K.P. 10 9 8 7 6 5 4 3 2 1

Contents

PREFACE 6

CHAPTER ONE

Origins 8

Planetary Percussion 11
The Emergence of Rhythm 13
Creation and Sound 16
Origin Stories 20
The Origins of Music 30
Early Instruments 31
Noise and Pandemonium 40

CHAPTER TWO

Rhythms of Work, War, and Play 46

Work 49
Communication 52
Hortators 55
Early War 56
Modern War 70
Play 74

CHAPTER THREE

Rhythms of Life and Death 100

Bacchanal 103
Psalms and Revelations 106
Masked Dance 110
The Dance of Death 112
Trance 118
Stillness 122
Shaman's Drum 125

Shaman's Rattle 130
Sacrifice 134
Possession 138
Carnaval! 140

CHAPTER FOUR

Sculptures of Sound 144

Membranophones 147
Making the Drum 152
Bullroarers 154
Idiophones 156
Bells, Voices of Metal 162
Skulls 170

CHAPTER FIVE

Planet Drum 172

South and Central America 175
Europe and North America 178
The Near East 188
Africa 190
Asia and Oceania 197
Children 208
Planet Drum 211

BIBLIOGRAPHY 214

DISCOGRAPHY 217

ACKNOWLEDGMENTS 218

CREDITS 219

INDEX 221

Preface

For forty years, since I was six, percussion has been my ruling passion, first as a player, then as a collector, and finally as a student. Ten years ago, hoping to answer certain questions I had about my chosen instrument, the drum, I embarked upon what I thought would be a simple research project. Although I had never been much of a reader of books or a taker of notes, I eagerly acquired these new skills, only to discover that the task I'd set myself was not as simple as I'd thought.

The mystery of the drum was deeper and more complex than I'd supposed. My first book, *Drumming at the Edge of Magic,* revealed some of what I discovered when I began to delve into that mystery.

My quests, in which I was aided by a resourceful team of fellow drum enthusiasts, led me back to the caves of the Paleolithic, to that moment when the rhythmic striking of stick against stick or stone against stone was perceived in a new and powerful light, and the art of percussion was born. It took me across the Siberian land bridge and down into the New World, leading from the tribes of North America, with their single and double membrane drums, to the jungle cultures of Amazonia, where the rattle is king.

Drumming — the rhythmic manipulation of noise — led me everywhere on the planet.

It introduced me to the lineage of drummers — my lineage — which is as old as any other in music. Through my research I met the frame drummers of ancient Sumeria and the Kaluli drummers of present-day Papua New Guinea, who hear in the sound of their drums the voices of the dead calling out to the living. It introduced me to shamans who used the drum as a trance tool that, like a horse, carried them out of their bodies to the World Tree; and to master drummers of West Africa who specialized in the ancient possession trance rhythms that called the ancestor spirits — the *Orisha* — down into the bodies of the dancers.

The drum led me back to the sacred, to ritual, to the mythic structures that underlie consciousness.

It consumed ten years of my life, but I never thought twice about expending my time and energy in this way. I was too excited and enriched by the extraordinary information that was flowing into my life. I wanted to hold this information in my hands, to play with it all the time. At first this was difficult since most of this information was stored in file folders and notebooks. But then one day I went out and bought several dozen four-by-eight-foot sheets of pegboard, which I arranged along the

And now nothing but drums…

OSCAR HIJUELOS,
THE MAMBO KINGS PLAY
SONGS OF LOVE

walls of the converted cow barn that was my headquarters during this period of my life. It took me only a couple of months to cover both sides with notes and pictures. I even installed special lights so I could work on any part of this expanding archive whenever I wanted.

It was difficult not to personify this pegboard creature that was now sharing my life. Perhaps because of its sinuous shape I saw it as a kind of snake, a big Anaconda that lived off of information. I loved to browse along its length, snapping on the lights to examine this or that section. I rarely was sequential in my perusal; I almost never started at the head and worked my way to the tail.

But then a day came when the pegboard snake was no longer sufficient to the task at hand. Too much information was coming in. A friend suggested I transfer my archive onto floppy disks, and so the Anaconda was dismantled and transformed into bits and bytes. But even in this new cybernetic form it retained a unique personality, becoming a kind of information tree with endlessly branching branches. I hired typists to keep up with the information flow and at night I would climb around in the upper branches, scanning for new and interesting growth.

The snake and the tree. Writing it down like this I see that the images have a kind of mythical resonance, recalling those old, old images of the World Tree in the Garden of Eden, with the snake twined around its trunk. Each way of dealing with this material had its strengths and weaknesses. The snake, for example, was perfect for displaying the pictures of the drum that I was so feverishly collecting, but it was less suited to carrying the quotes and anecdotes, the lengthy origin myths and anthropological fieldwork — the written legacy of the drum. For this the computer and its information tree proved superior, but unfortunately the technology was not yet in place that would have allowed me to bring images into this domain.

With *Drumming at the Edge of Magic* and now *Planet Drum,* my obsession has assumed a third form — the book — and in many ways it strikes me as the best. Here are the images that made the Anaconda come alive those nights when I wandered its length in the Barn, combined with the tastiest fruits that grew on my information tree. You can read it cover to cover, as if you're following a kind of march beat, or you can find your own rhythm and dance your own dance through the images and ideas that you find on the following pages.

But before you begin, let me place a few thoughts in the forefront of your consciousness. It's said in different places in different ways: In ancient China, Confucius said that music is basic to human nature. In Africa today they say that a village without music is a dead place. In most Western popular music, spontaneity has been lost in favor of preprogrammed offerings. World music — and the percussive impulse that drives it — reaches past the need of the marketplace to sell, into emotional and spiritual dialogue with older oral traditions.

What we call world music really is all the world's music. It's a reflection of our dreams, our lives, and it represents every fiber of our beings. It's an aural soundscape, a language of the deepest emotions; it's what we sound like as a people. The excitement that we feel when we hear it tells us that the door into the realm of the spirit is opening. It's a romance of the ear. It's our musical skeleton key.

Underneath the world's extraordinary musical diversity is another, deeper realm in which there is no better or worse, no modern or primitive, no art music versus folk music, no distinctions at all, but rather an almost organic compulsion to translate the emotional fact of being alive into sound, into rhythm, into something you can dance to.

MICKEY HART

CHAPTER ONE

ORIGINS

The loudest sound in the neighborhood is heard after lightning arches between clouds and earth, superheating and expanding the air along its length, a compression or shock wave that decays to become what we call thunder. Lightning bridges the gap between heaven and earth.

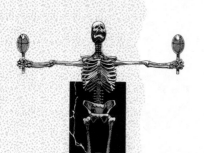

THE SOUND HAS BEEN CALLED MANY THINGS BY many cultures. Some call it the seed sound, the One, the pulse at the heart of the universe. The Hindus call it the Nada Brahma; we prefer the big bang. *In the beginning was the noise.* One of the few fundamental things we know about our universe is that everything in it is vibrating, is in motion, has a rhythm. Every molecule, every atom is dancing its own unique dance, singing its signature song. What we call sight is just the limited spectrum of vibrations that our eyes can perceive; what we call sound is just the limited spectrum of pulsations that our ears can hear. *And this noise begat rhythm and rhythm begat everything else.* This is a story about the discovery, somewhere in the mists of time, that we, the small apelike creature Homo sapiens, could master and manipulate noise to create our own rhythms, and about the extraordinary tools we developed to explore this discovery. This is a story about drums and drumming, and about the primal experience of *percussion.* You don't simply play a drum, you *beat* it, you *strike* it, you *pound* it, the vibration, contraction, and expansion of the membrane giving off a roar that contains an echo of that other roar, fifteen to twenty billion years ago, when the universe, packed into an extremely dense area of matter and energy, suddenly exploded. *And the dance began.*

Planetary Percussion

A sound precipitates air, then fire, then water and earth — and that's how the world becomes. The whole universe is included in this first sound, this vibration, which then commits all things to fragmentation in the field of time. In this view, there is not someone outside who said, "Let it happen."

JOSEPH CAMPBELL

The beginning of our universe: mysterious forces came together and space, matter, and time began, with a vibration unlike anything before or since. The big bang, a birth in chaos and din, was beat one.

TIMELINE
Dates are approximate

15-20 billion years ago

The big bang

5 billion years ago

Our planet forms

3 billion years ago

Life begins on earth

450 million years ago

First life on land

70 million years ago

First mammals

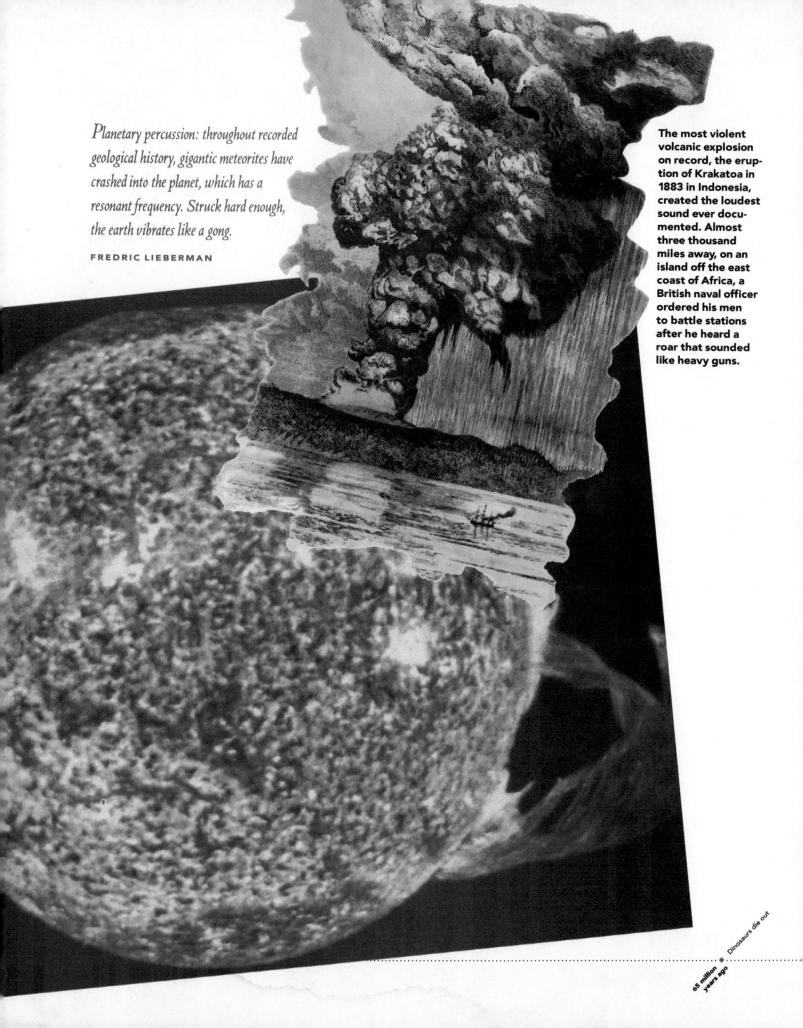

Planetary percussion: throughout recorded geological history, gigantic meteorites have crashed into the planet, which has a resonant frequency. Struck hard enough, the earth vibrates like a gong.

FREDRIC LIEBERMAN

The most violent volcanic explosion on record, the eruption of Krakatoa in 1883 in Indonesia, created the loudest sound ever documented. Almost three thousand miles away, on an island off the east coast of Africa, a British naval officer ordered his men to battle stations after he heard a roar that sounded like heavy guns.

65 million years ago ■ Dinosaurs die out

The Emergence of Rhythm

Early humans no doubt were awed and terrified by the wild percussive noise of nature – the volcanoes, the thunderstorms – and early percussion instruments may have been a way of approximating and therefore taming this terrifying sound.

But gentler models also may have contributed to the development of percussion. The gorilla beating on its chest is an example of body percussion known to even the smallest child. And what of the beaver slapping its tail on the water to warn other beavers of danger? Or spiders that drum on their webs, or termites that hammer the ground as they march? If we examine closely the myths of the origins of percussion instruments, what stands out is how rigorously and accurately our ancestors observed nature and how playfully they applied the lessons learned there.

Instrumental music...began in general as a percussive act of the body: slapping the buttocks, the belly, the thighs, or clapping the hands, or stamping the ground.

CURT SACHS

To hone the fine cutting edges of a hand axe or other rudimentary tool requires repeated rhythmic movements by the toolmaker.

Australopithecines were our earliest ancestors who walked erect as we do. They lived between eight million and one and a half million years ago. We cannot pinpoint the moment when music began, but evidence suggests that these hominids used repeated rhythmic movements to fashion stone tools.

5–10 million years ago • Earliest protohominids

2,500,000 years ago • Stones used as tools

1,600,000 years ago • Crafted tools

400,000 years ago • Homo sapiens appears

60,000 years ago • Development of complex tools

50,000 years ago • Humans first cross land bridge from Asia to North America

Hunting bows, musical bows

Earliest known cave paintings

KALYNN

The British biologist Sir Julian Huxley (1887–1975) wrote of an African trip, "I remember waking up at night at camp, near Lake Edward in the Belgian Congo, and hearing a strange clicking or ticking sound. A flashlight revealed that this was emanating from a column of termites which was crossing the floor of the tent under cover of darkness."

When I hear the humming of the little world among the stalks, and am near the countless indescribable forms of the worms and insects, then I feel the presence of the Almighty, who created us in His own image.

JOHANN WOLFGANG VON GOETHE

Upper Paleolithic period begins (through 10,000 years ago)

35,000 years ago

Idiophones, rattles, and such)

Bone flutes

Body percussion. The mountain gorilla beats his chest rhythmically, making a hollow, booming sound to declare his presence or intimidate potential intruders.

A bronze Shiva Nataraja plays an hourglass drum upraised in one of his right hands and dances, thus creating the world. In his left hand he holds the flame of destruction that will end this age. Hindus believe that as long as Shiva dances, the world will continue to exist. If and when this dance stops, all life shall return into Shiva's essence. [South India, ca. 990 A.D.]

Creation and Sound

Rhythm and noise.

Many of the world's cosmologies associate the beginning (and the end) of time with loud, percussive noise – the new, the unexpected. Noise is raw sound.

Rhythm is anything that repeats itself in time: the moon cycling around the earth, the sap rising in the spring, the pulsing of arteries in the body.

Science knows one big thing about rhythm, something it calls the law of entrainment. Discovered by the Dutch scientist Christian Huygens in 1665, the law of entrainment holds that if two rhythms are nearly the same and their sources are in close proximity, they will always lock up, fall into synchrony, entrain. Why? The best theory is that nature is efficient and it takes less energy to pulse together than in opposition.

Because we are a part of nature, it is likely that we are entrained with the larger planetary and universal rhythms that surround us.

Our word *religion* comes from the Latin and means "to bind together." A successful religion is one that binds together all the fundamental rhythms that each of us experiences: the personal rhythm of the human body, the larger social rhythm of the family, tribe, or nation, and the enveloping cosmic rhythms of the planet and universe. If a religion "works," its followers are rewarded by a new dimension of rhythm and time – the sacred.

Creation in Hinduism depends on the five elements of ether, air, fire, water, earth. The first is ether, and ether is sound — the original sound, the nada. *Out of the vibrations of* nada *comes the universe. That's the beginning of the universe — it begins with sound, vibrations.*

And sound is also used to conjure up a deity. In the beginning was the Word, the voice. When you are summoning a deity, you pronounce the seed syllable of the holy name.

JOSEPH CAMPBELL

In Chinese mythology, P'an-ku figures as the "great architect" of the universe. Pounding and chiseling upon the cliffs of Chaos, he sculpted the stars and planets, a labor that took eighteen thousand years. When he vanished, suffering began on earth.

In this Ethiopian Coptic illumination of the Bible's Revelation of Saint John the Divine, the drummers in the heavens sound the end of the world, playing kettledrums with curved sticks. [Anonymous Ethiopian artist, eighteenth century]

And out of the throne proceeded lightnings and thunderings and voices: and there were seven lamps of fire burning before the throne, which are the seven Spirits of God.

REVELATION 4:5

Planet Drum

18

In the beginning was the Word, and the Word was with God, and the Word was God.

JOHN 1:1

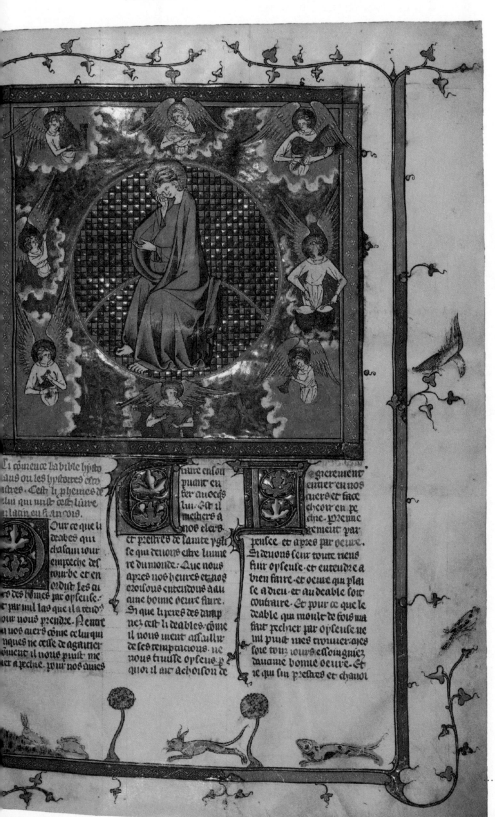

The spirit of Logos (Greek for "word") is surrounded by angels in a heavenly orchestra celebrating the creation. One angel plays two small kettledrums while another rings a bell. [*The Logos Seated on the Rainbow*, anonymous French artist, early fourteenth century]

Origin Stories

MORGON-KARA

SIBERIA ～ BURIAT PEOPLE

Mythology is what happened, is happening and will happen to us all, from the very beginning until the end of human life upon the earth.

BARBARA TUCHMAN

The Buriat of Irkutsk (Siberia) . . . declare that Morgon-Kara, their first shaman, was so competent that he could bring back souls from the dead. And so the Lord of the Dead complained to the High God of Heaven, and God decided to pose the shaman a test. He got possession of the soul of a certain man and slipped it into a bottle, covering the opening with the ball of his thumb. The man grew ill, and his relatives sent for Morgon-Kara. The shaman looked everywhere for the missing soul. He searched the forest, the waters, the mountain gorges, the land of the dead, and at last mounted, sitting on his drum, to the world above, where again he was forced to search for a long time. ～ Presently he observed that the High God of Heaven was keeping a bottle covered with the ball of his thumb and, studying the circumstance, perceived that inside the bottle was the very soul he had come to find. The wily shaman changed himself into a wasp. He flew at God and gave him such a hot sting on the forehead than the thumb jerked from the opening and the captive got away. ～ Then the next thing God knew, there was this shaman, Morgon-Kara, sitting on his drum again, and going down to earth with the recovered soul. The flight in this case, however, was not entirely successful. Becoming terribly angry, God immediately diminished the power of the shaman forever by splitting his drum in two. ～ And so that is why from that day to this, shaman drums, which originally were fitted with two heads of skin, have had only one.

HOW UNIVERSE, THE SUPREME BEING, MAKES RAIN

SIBERIA ⁓ KORYAK PEOPLE

One time, when Big Raven was living on earth, it rained for so long that his underground house filled with water, and everything he owned got wet and began to rot. ⁓ "Universe must be doing something up there," Big Raven said to his eldest son, Ememqut. "Let's fly up and see." ⁓ They went outside, put on their raven coats and flew to Universe's place. As they got near, they could hear the sound of drumming. It was Universe who was drumming, with his wife, Rain Woman, at his side. Universe had cut off Rain Woman's vulva and hung it on his drum. He was using his own penis as a drumstick. Whenever he beat the drum, water poured from Rain Woman's vulva like rain. ⁓ When Universe saw Big Raven, he quickly hid the drum and the rain stopped. ⁓ "The rain has stopped," Big Raven said to Ememqut. "We can leave." ⁓ As soon as they left, the drumming began again and the rain started to fall. So Big Raven and his son turned right around and went back, and as soon as Universe saw them he again hid the drum and the rain stopped. This time Big Raven whispered to his son, "We'll pretend to go, but instead we'll hide and see what they are doing." ⁓ Big Raven and his son disguised themselves as two reindeer hairs and lay on the floor and watched as Universe asked his wife for the drum which she took from the secret hiding place. As soon as Universe began to play, it began to rain as hard as before. ⁓ Big Raven said to Ememqut, "I'm going to make them fall asleep. You watch where they put the drum and the stick." ⁓ He made a sleeping spell, and Universe and his wife fell into a deep sleep. Then Big Raven took the drum and the drumstick from their secret hiding places and roasted them over the fire until both were dry and crisp. Then he returned them and broke the sleeping spell. Immediately Universe picked up his drum and began to beat on it, only this time the more he beat it the finer the weather became, until there wasn't a cloud in the sky. Then Universe and his wife went to bed. ⁓ "Now," Big Raven said to Ememqut, "let us really go home." ⁓ The wonderful fine weather lasted for days, but the hunting was terrible. No one had any luck hunting reindeer or sea mammals. Everyone began to starve because Universe was asleep. ⁓ "I'm going up there to see what's going on," Big Raven said. He put on his raven coat and flew up to Universe's place to talk with him. "We're having very good weather," he told Universe, "but everybody's starving. We can't find any game." ⁓ "That's because I'm not looking after my children," Universe replied. "Go back home. From now on you'll have good hunting." ⁓ So Big Raven left and when his sons next went hunting they found sea mammals and wild reindeer. And when Big Raven himself pulled from the ground the post to which his dogs were tied, out came a whole herd of reindeer. Many of these he sacrificed to Universe, and after that he had only good luck with his hunting.

God created the wooden drum. It belonged to a large genie with one eye, one arm, and one leg, whose village was in a termite hill. This genie chopped down trees and cleared the brush, and in the center of this open space he set the wooden drum. ❧ One day an orphan left his village and went into the bush. Arriving at the genie's clearing he spotted the wooden drum. Two sticks were lying on it. The boy took the sticks and began to beat the wooden drum. ❧ A genie stuck his head out of the termite mound and said, "Who told you to beat the wooden drum?" ❧ "No one told me," answered the boy. ❧ "Since you have already started to beat the drum," said the genie, "continue so that I may dance. If I dance and my feet get tired, you can kill me. But if my feet don't tire and your hands do, then I'll kill you." ❧ The young boy beat on the wooden drum. The genie danced. When he got tired he went on the other side of the termite mound and a fresh genie popped out and resumed dancing. Eventually the boy tired and the genie killed him. ❧ Now this boy, though an orphan, had a younger brother. For three days the brother waited in the village for his older brother to return. When he didn't, the younger boy decided to go look for him. When he arrived at the genie's clearing, he saw the wooden drum and beside it the severed head of his brother. "What! Is this the head of my brother?" he said. "And what's this wooden thing on the ground with the two pretty sticks on it?" The younger brother picked up the sticks and began to beat on the drum. ❧ Immediately a genie appeared and said, "Go ahead, beat on that drum while I dance. But if your hands get tired before my feet do, I will kill you." ❧ The young man beat the drum; the genie danced and danced. ❧ But he did something his brother didn't do. Whenever the genie danced around to the other side of the termite mound, the boy went with him. They circled for a long time. Finally the genie said, "My foot is tired. I'm going to dance with my shoulder." ❧ The genie danced with his shoulder until that got tired. Then he danced with his neck. When that got tired he shook his arm. Then he said, "This is the day when it will happen." ❧ "When what will happen?" asked the boy. ❧ "I am tired all over, what more can I say?" said the genie. ❧ Then the boy said, "The day has arrived for me to avenge the death of my older brother, whose head lies here in the dirt. I don't fear you." ❧ He killed the genie. Then he went around to the other side of the termite hill and set it on fire. All the genies died. ❧ Picking up the wooden drum, the young man returned to his village.

THE ORIGIN OF THE WOODEN DRUM

AFRICA ❧ DAN PEOPLE

It is told that the Great Ancestors hid the gift of their voices inside the wood of trees, so that men and women could call them whenever they needed to. But the first men and women were ignorant of this one last gift; they knew nothing about it. ❧ Now it happened that the first men and women were

BULLROARER COMES TO THE PEOPLE

AUSTRALIA

undergoing a terrible famine. Food and even water were scarce. One day an old woman was out cutting firewood when suddenly the splinters from the tree she was felling began to fly around her in the air, crying, "Bigu-bigu-bigu-bigu." ❧ It frightened the old woman very much. When she told her husband what had happened he said that whatever the thing was it would come to her that night in a dream. And sure enough, it did. That night, as the old woman slept, one of the wood chips came to her and said: ❧ "Mother, listen to me. Bigu is my name. That's my name, Bigu! Now I want you to go into the bush and cut a long skin from a tree and make a rope. Then I want you to make a hole close to my nose, and fasten the rope there. Then, mother, plant yams. Then I want you to sling me over your

head. The noise I make will make your garden grow. It will make the wind and the rain come. It will wake up the ground." ❧ Well, the old woman did as Bigu commanded. She found a tree, she made a rope, she hitched it to the splinter, she planted yams, and then she began to swing Bigu over her head. ❧ It sounded like a great monster had come to eat them all up. The ground moved. The first people ran and hid under the bushes, screaming, "Dhuramoolan has come to eat us." ❧ The old woman called to the people, "Come back! You feel the rain fall? This water is for us to drink. You see the yams grow? Now we have food!" ❧ The people gathered around her, their eyes wide with fear and wonder. Everywhere the yams were growing and the rain was falling. Oh, the people were happy. ❧ But not the husband of the old woman. Angrily he snatched the bullroarer from his wife and killed her. Then he painted himself with white clay as if he were about to kill a strong enemy. He picked up his spear and called the men to him and said, "All you men, this Bigu gives us power. No longer will women and children be allowed to see it. Only men. Not boys, not girls, not women. This magic is too strong. If any man tells the women and children about this, I will kill him." ❧ The man, who was now the chief, swung the bullroarer. The people were frightened by the tremendous noise. Some ran and hid under trees or in water holes. Then the chief called the boys who were old enough to be husbands and men. He put them in a big hole, saying they would be eaten by Dhuramoolan. He made their mothers and the little children lie next to the hole on some brush. As the bullroarer howled above them, the mothers clung tight to the belts of their sons. But not tight enough. Gradually each of the boys pulled away from their mothers, and was not seen again for a long long time. ❧ When they did return, they were men.

Here is the story of the beginning of the ceremonial powwow drum. It was the first time when the white soldiers massacred the Indians when this Sioux woman gave four sons of hers to fight for her people. But she lost her four sons in this massacre and ran away after she knew her people were losing the war. The soldiers were after her but she ran into a lake. . . . She went in the water and hid under the lily pads. While she was there, the Great Spirit came and spoke to her and told her, "There is only one thing for you to do." ☙ It took four days to tell her. It was windy and the wind flipped the lily pads so she could breathe and look to see if anyone was around. No – the sound was all that she made out, but from it she remembered all the Great Spirit told her. On the fourth day at noon she came out and went to her people to see what was left from the war. . . . The Great Spirit told her what to do: "Tell your people, if there are any left [and he told her there were], you tell your people to make a drum and tell them what I told you." The Great Spirit taught her also the songs she knew and she told the men folks how to sing the songs. "It will be the only way you are going to stop the soldiers from killing your people." ☙ So her people did what she said, and when the soldiers who were massacring

the Indians heard the sound of the drum, they put down their arms, stood still, and stopped the killing, and to this day white people are always wanting to see a powwow. ☙ This powwow drum is called in English "Sioux drum," in Ojibwa

THE VISION OF TAILFEATHER WOMAN

NORTH AMERICA ☙ SIOUX PEOPLE

bwaanidewe'igan. It was put here on earth before peace terms were made with the whites. After the whites saw what the Indians were doing, how they were having a good time and had no time to fight, the white man didn't fight. After all this took place the whites made peace terms with the Indians. So the Indians kept on the powwow. It's because the Sioux woman lost her four sons in the war that the Great Spirit came upon her and told her to make the drum to show that the Indians had power too, which they keep secret.

The Origins of Music

Numerous theories try to explain the origin of music. Some have us learning to sing by mimicking the mating calls of birds and animals, while others suggest that music grew out of our discovery that sounds of a single pitch carry a long way, thus making group communication much easier. At some point in our development, early humans began accompanying these songs with simple instruments, concussion sticks and beaters, on which they produced that special kind of vibration, that sharp shock of percussive noise.

As toolmakers we were busy scraping, striking, rubbing, shaking, swinging — verbs that perfectly describe the class of percussion instruments known as idiophones. The bodily rhythms and the percussive payoff are similar; only the context separates the striking of two flints to make a spearhead from the whacking of two sticks to make a rhythm — sound tools.

Ethnomusicologist John Blacking believed there was a connection between our rapid evolution as a species and our ability to recognize, externalize, and control rhythms. For Blacking, the tool record — all those delicately chipped arrowheads and choppers — was a dramatic illustration of our battle to master the subtle bodily rhythms that the creation of any advanced technology requires.

Blacking also believed that music was a special case. It wasn't just another example of our ability to master rhythm; it was the mystery of rhythm *itself*. Music was a mirror that reflected a culture's deepest social and biological rhythms, an externalization of the pulses that remained hidden beneath the busyness of daily life.

Philosopher Suzanne Langer has speculated that music, language, and dance originated together in the very earliest rituals — people gathering together, dancing, and singing.

Naturalist Charles Darwin linked the origin of music with sex: music evolved from mating calls of birds and animals.

Economist Karl Bücher argued that rhythm developed from the need to coordinate large groups of people working together at lifting, breaking, dragging things — requiring maximum group effort exerted at the same moment.

Psychologist Karl Stumpf suggested that the idea of singing on clear pitches perhaps developed because loud singing has much greater carrying power than speech or shouts.

Philosopher Herbert Spencer supported the idea that people tend to exaggerate the expressive vocalizations in their language when in highly emotional states, leading to wails or shouts that could have become stylized and thus musical.

Anthropologist Siegfried Nadel proposed that music developed as an enhanced mode of communication with supernatural powers.

When struck, the stalactites in the caves of Dordogne sound like gongs or bells. More than ten thousand years ago the caves were holy to the people who lived nearby, as the extraordinary paintings found inside them demonstrate. [Pech-Merle, France]

8000 B.C.

Neolithic period (to 1500 B.C.)

First Fertile Crescent village settlements

Beginning of bronze technology

Domestication of plants

Skin-covered drums (membranophones)

Early Instruments

The rhythmic manipulation of noise is one of our earliest accomplishments, predating by millennia the discovery of the wheel and the plow. Starting with concussion sticks, hollow logs, sounding bows, and eventually skin drums, we have carried this knowledge with us on our long migrations.

We find percussion everywhere on this planet, yet nowhere is it exactly the same. Each culture brought its own genius, its own materials, to the task of rhythm making. Traveling through time and across space, we can chart these transformations as the rhythm slowly came forth from the human body and took up residence in stone, metal, skin, wood, and bone.

The importance of this transformation is underscored by the instruments themselves. Even today, hundreds of years after many of them were carefully crafted, they still manage to convey the understanding that they were both functional musical instruments and sacred tools.

This Neolithic pottery drum was unearthed in Germany. It may have been modeled on an earlier wooden drum. [Germany, ca. 2500 B.C.]

A contemporary Australian aborigine (right) plays concussion or clapper sticks, among the most ancient of instruments, while his companion creates a drone and melody on the *didjeridu*. [Arnhem Land, Australia, twentieth century] ▼

▲ The first instruments may have been gathered, not made: found objects. Among the Kabre of West Africa today, young boys play rocks to mark important times in the agricultural cycle. [Togo, 1960s]

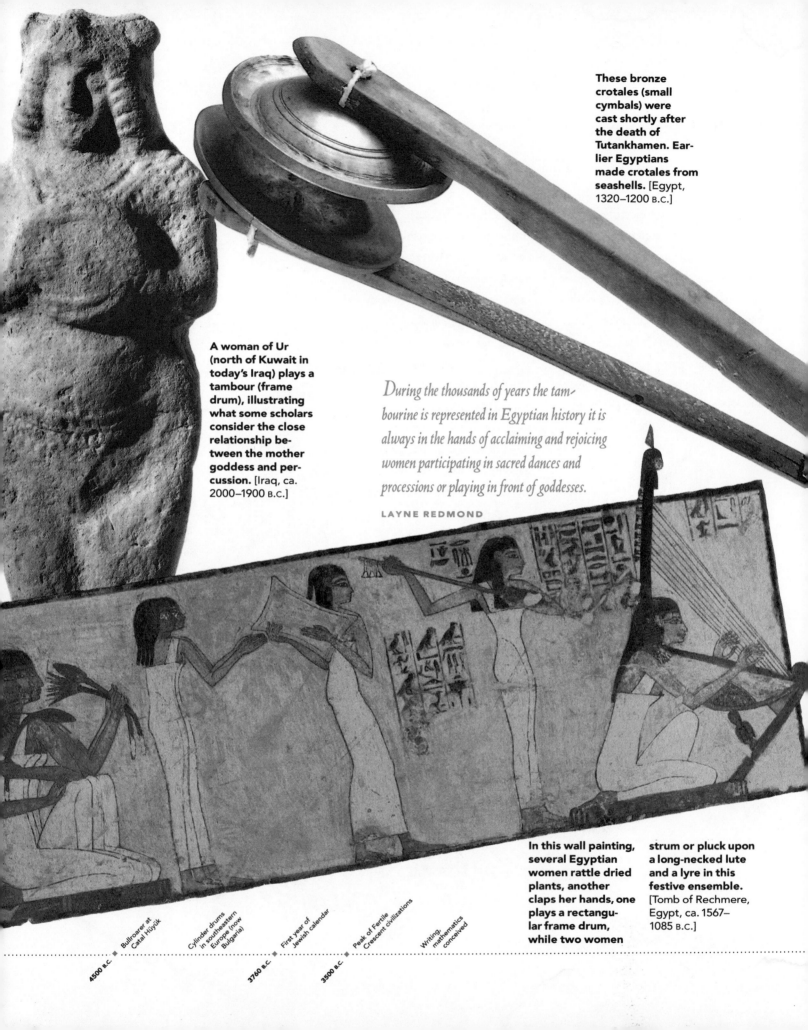

These bronze crotales (small cymbals) were cast shortly after the death of Tutankhamen. Earlier Egyptians made crotales from seashells. [Egypt, 1320–1200 B.C.]

A woman of Ur (north of Kuwait in today's Iraq) plays a tambour (frame drum), illustrating what some scholars consider the close relationship between the mother goddess and percussion. [Iraq, ca. 2000–1900 B.C.]

During the thousands of years the tambourine is represented in Egyptian history it is always in the hands of acclaiming and rejoicing women participating in sacred dances and processions or playing in front of goddesses.

LAYNE REDMOND

In this wall painting, several Egyptian women rattle dried plants, another claps her hands, one plays a rectangular frame drum, while two women strum or pluck upon a long-necked lute and a lyre in this festive ensemble. [Tomb of Rechmere, Egypt, ca. 1567–1085 B.C.]

4500 B.C. ■ Bullroarer at Catal Hüyük

Cylinder drums in southeastern Europe (now Bulgaria)

3760 B.C. ■ First year of Jewish calendar

3500 B.C. ■ Peak of Fertile Crescent civilizations

Writing, mathematics conceived

Two musicians play an enormous frame drum while another blows a ram's horn. [Mesopotamia, ca. 1000 B.C.]

Elaborately carved from wood or ivory in the shape of human arms and hands, Egyptian clappers were often associated with the worship of Isis, the great mother goddess. Surviving painting and pottery, dating as early as the fourth millennium B.C., depicts the use of clappers in fertility and harvest rites.

In ancient Egypt, a rattle of wood or metal (called a sistrum) was used to ward off evil spirits and attract the attention of beneficent forces. [Egypt, 2133–730 B.C.] ▼

The sacred sistrum is most often played by women in ritual devotion to the mother goddess called Isis, Hathor, Bast, or Astarte. [Egypt, 2133–730 B.C.]

Drums move from Fertile Crescent to Far East (China)

Dancing figures with drums hunt and perform ritual sacrifice. Dozens of cliff paintings such as these illustrate the daily lives of these makers of bronze drums who lived in south central China. [China, 475 B.C. – 220 A.D.]

This rubbing of a tomb wall shows an ancient measuring device. As the chariot's wheels turned, the mechanical drummers struck the barrel drum, measuring the distance traveled by the number of beats. [China, 128 A.D.]

Music rises from the human heart. When the emotions are touched, they are expressed in sounds, and when the sounds take definite forms, we have music. Therefore the music of a peaceful and

These glazed earthenware drummers represent the entourage of a noble, and were buried with him to serve in death. The drums would aid the noble's spirit guardians in battles of the afterlife. Burying clay models substituted for an earlier practice of burying the servants themselves. [China, ca. 600 A.D.]

prosperous country is quiet and joyous, and the government is orderly; the music of a country in turmoil shows dissatisfaction and anger, and the government is chaotic; and the music of a destroyed country shows sorrow and remembrance of the past, and the people are distressed. Thus we see music and government are directly connected with one another.

CHINESE CLASSIC

This clay tomb figurine depicts a singer/storyteller accompanying himself on a small drum. Similar solo drumming and singing continues to the present day in China. [China, 25–200 A.D.]

2000 B.C. — Kurgans (Indo-Europeans) sweep southward   1500 B.C. — Rise of Vedic religion   1200 B.C. — Rise of Dionysian religion   1100 B.C. — Bronze drums in China   1000 B.C. — Large-scale slash-and-burn agriculture   Kettledrums in Babylonia and India

A bronze statuette found in North Africa depicts a woman dancing with crotales in her hands. [Tunisia, ca. 100 B.C.]

In this medieval European woodcut, the Roman philosopher Boethius plays a monochord (a single-stringed instrument). [Detail from Boethius's *De Musica*, Canterbury, England, 1150 A.D.]

800 B.C. ◆ Rise of Apollonian religion

700 B.C. ◆ Drums in Babylonia

600 B.C. ◆ Rise of Hinduism

628–551 B.C. ◆ Zoroaster

563–483 B.C. ◆ Buddha

551–479 B.C. ◆ Confucius

470–399 B.C. ◆ Socrates

A singing woman shakes a gourd rattle. Voluptuous feminine imagery found in the New World may be rooted in the ancient mother goddess traditions of the Old World. [Mexico, 300–1000 A.D.]

This bottle is a one-man band with panpipes, drum, and some sort of ear trumpet coming from the left side of his head. The figure's costume is covered with pan-pipe designs, which are often seen in the art of the period. [Peru, 100 A.D.]

A circle of dancers with drummer in the center is frozen in clay. [Nayarit people, Mexico, 200 B.C.– 400 A.D.]

A tortoiseshell makes a fine percussion instrument; its hollow body resonates when the elastic underbelly is struck. The notched surface may also be scraped. [Zapotec people, Mexico, 600 A.D.]

These two clay figures of drummer and acrobat were found together at an archeological site. [Mexico, 600–1000 A.D.]

Origins

37

356–323 B.C. — Alexander the Great

4 B.C. — Birth of Christ; Christian era begins

500 A.D. — Kurgan expansion into West Africa (to 1000 A.D.)

570–632 — Muhammad (rise of Islam)

900 — Viking settlements in North America

1095 — First Crusade

1100 — Barrel drum introduced in Europe

1300 — Side drum introduced in Europe

Turkish Janissary bands (abolished in 1826)

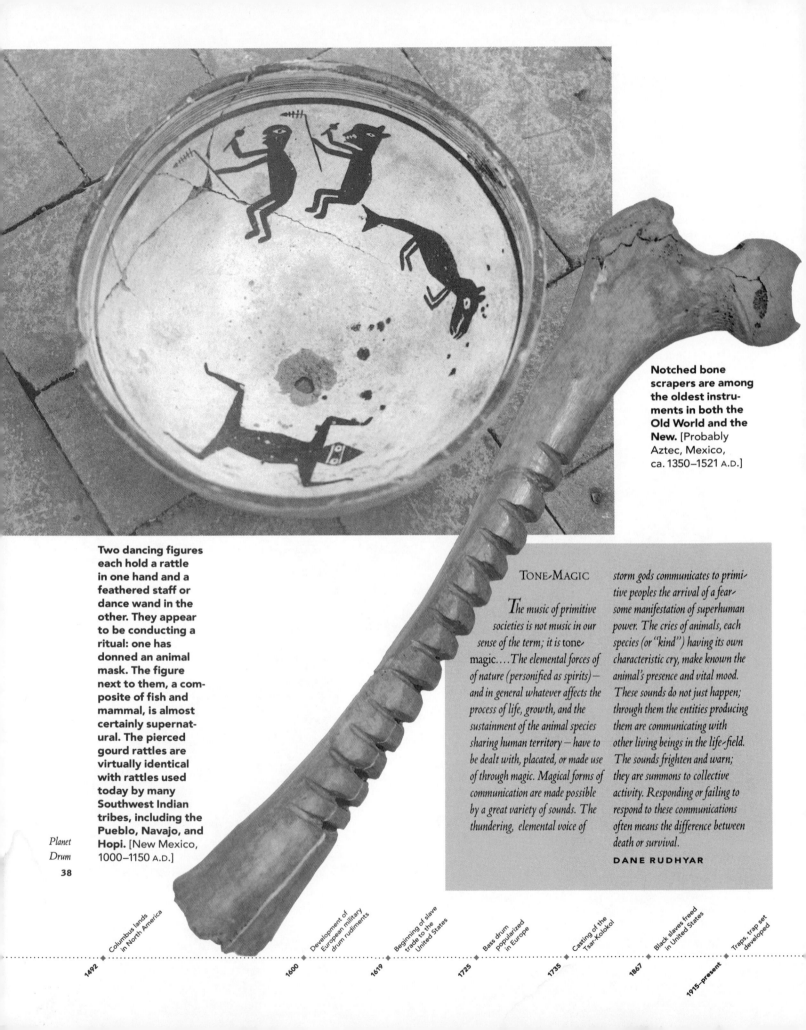

Notched bone scrapers are among the oldest instruments in both the Old World and the New. [Probably Aztec, Mexico, ca. 1350–1521 A.D.]

Two dancing figures each hold a rattle in one hand and a feathered staff or dance wand in the other. They appear to be conducting a ritual: one has donned an animal mask. The figure next to them, a composite of fish and mammal, is almost certainly supernatural. The pierced gourd rattles are virtually identical with rattles used today by many Southwest Indian tribes, including the Pueblo, Navajo, and Hopi. [New Mexico, 1000–1150 A.D.]

Planet Drum

38

TONE·MAGIC

The music of primitive societies is not music in our sense of the term; it is tone-magic....The elemental forces of of nature (personified as spirits)— and in general whatever affects the process of life, growth, and the sustainment of the animal species sharing human territory — have to be dealt with, placated, or made use of through magic. Magical forms of communication are made possible by a great variety of sounds. The thundering, elemental voice of storm gods communicates to primitive peoples the arrival of a fearsome manifestation of superhuman power. The cries of animals, each species (or "kind") having its own characteristic cry, make known the animal's presence and vital mood. These sounds do not just happen; through them the entities producing them are communicating with other living beings in the life-field. The sounds frighten and warn; they are summons to collective activity. Responding or failing to respond to these communications often means the difference between death or survival.

DANE RUDHYAR

1492 — Columbus lands in North America

1600 — Development of European military drum rudiments

1619 — Beginning of slave trade to the United States

1725 — Bass drum Popularized in Europe

1735 — Casting of the Tsar-Kolokol

1867 — Black slaves freed in United States

1915–present — Traps, trap set developed

A seated musician-priest plays a jaguar-skin covered *huehuetl* for Xochi-pilli, the rattle-carrying Aztec god of dance and festival. [Mexico, six-teenth century A.D.]

A pottery fragment, attributed to the Hohokam, a people who lived in the area now known as Arizona, shows several dancers with large gourd rattles and leg rattles. [700–1200 A.D.]

A *teponaztli* was carved in the form of a coyote with ivory teeth. In Aztec myth, the coyote was related to the moon and stars. [Aztec people, Mexico, ca. 1500 A.D.]

Origins

39

Noise and Pandemonium

Rhythm and noise – there isn't a culture on the planet that hasn't reached some accommodation with these two elemental forces. Some cultures are ecstatically rhythmic and percussive; others are almost the opposite, preferring subdued rhythms and sweet melody. In China during Confucian times, music was thought to be a direct reflection of the people's spirit. Noisy, ribald music signified an unruly government, frowned upon in a culture that valued calmness and serenity.

A similar antipathy for ecstatic rhythm and percussive noise characterized the Christian Middle Ages. Sacred music was vocal music; in many places instrumental and dance music were forbidden. Outside of the military, where the drum played an important role in communication, drumming was seen as an aberration that signaled the presence of Satan, not godly grace. So strong was this bias that even after secular music achieved glorious expression in the orchestral works of Bach and Mozart, the drum was scarcely to be found in the orchestra. And when it did manage to gain a musical foothold in the nineteenth century, it was relegated to the rare flourish or thunderclap.

A delight in the complex rhythmic possibilities of noise did not return to the Christian West until the late nineteenth century, when in the New World the music of the recently freed West African slaves began to mutate into jazz, blues, rhythm and blues, and rock and roll.

A vision of hell as din and chaos. The instruments intended to delight and please the ear are turned through Hieronymus Bosch's diabolical artistic imagination into instruments of torture. Music invades these people. At lower right (and inset), one of Satan's demons batters a field drum, torturing an imprisoned sinner. [Details from *Garden of Earthly Delights*, Netherlands, 1510–1515]

In information theory, signal is the part of a message that carries meaning, and noise is the part that carries no signal. In other words, noise equals no-sense or nonsense. But today's signal will become, through the law of entropy (that says that every-thing is slowing down), tomor-row's noise, and, vice versa, today's noise will soon be enjoyed as tomorrow's signal.

FREDRIC LIEBERMAN

Demons and angels struggle for the possession of souls, accompanied by nakers (small kettle-drums) booming and long trumpets blaring. [Detail of *The Last Judg-ment,* by Stefan Lochner, Germany, ca. 1435–1440]

The everyday din of the London streets is a nightmare to the man who is trying to practice his violin. [*The Enraged Musician*, by William Hogarth, England, 1741]

The first reported poltergeist was a "demon drummer" in Tedworth, England, 1689.

A smoking pistol cools; one musician prepares to fire a cannon while another kneels, ready to bash a large metal washbucket. Many listeners thought musical pyrotechnics served noise rather than beauty, and did not like it when an expanded percussion ensemble was introduced into the Western orchestra in the late nineteenth century. They complained that it was too raw, too noisy, ugly, unmannered. [*Musique pyrotechnique, Charivarique et Diabolique*, by Honoré Daumier, France, 1838] ▼

Let's walk together through a great modern capital, with the ear more attentive than the eye, and we will vary the pleasures of our sensibilities by distinguishing among the gurglings of water, air, and gas inside metallic pipes, the rumbling and trattlings of engines beating with obvious animal spirits, the rising and falling of pistons, the stridency of mechanical saws, the loud jumping of trolleys on their rails, the snapping of whips, the shipping of flags. We will have fun imagining our orchestration of department stores' sliding doors, the hubbub of the crowds, the different roars of railroad stations, iron foundries, textile mills, printing houses, power plants, and subways. And we must not forget the very new noises of modern warfare.

LUIGI RUSSOLO

ise (nɔɪz), *sb.* Forms: 3-7 noyse, 4-6 noys, 5-6 yes, *Sc.* noyis, 6 noyse; 4 nois, 6 noiz, 3- noise. so 4 nouse, nowse, 5 nose. [a. F. *noise* (11th nt.; OF. also *noyse, nose*) = Prov. *noysa, nosa, usa*, of uncertain origin: L. *nausea* and *noxia* ve been proposed, but the sense of the word is ainst both suggestions.]

. a. Loud outcry, clamour, or shouting; din or turbance made by one or more persons.

n this and other senses freq. in the phrase *to make* (more ely †*keep*) *a noise*: cf. sense 6.

1225 *Ancren R.* 66 þe wreche peoddare more noise he keð to ȝeien his sope, þen a riche mercer al his deorewurðe re. **1297** R. GLOUC. (Rolls) 8167 Of trompes & of tabors sarazins made þere So gret noyse þat cristinemen al tourbed were. **a1300** *Cursor M.* 6535 He hard þe gret s was þare Abute þis calf. **c1330** R. BRUNNE *Chron. Wace* lls) 11531 At þat word was noise & cry Of þe Bretons þat den ney. ?**1370** *Robt. Cicyle* 174 (Horstm.), He gan crie make nois, He swor þei schulde alle abye [etc.]. **1390** WER *Conf.* III. 321 With this noise and with this cry, Out barge faste by.. Men sterten out. **1455** *Paston Lett.* I. They sette an hous on fyer.., and cryed and mad an se as though they had be sory for the fyer. **1481** CAXTON *ifrey* v. 23 Of the noyse that sourded emonge the hethen n discordyng in theyr lawe. **a1533** LD. BERNERS *Huon* lix. They all made great ioy with suche a ioyfull noyse that paynyms without dyd here it. **1590** SHAKS. *Com. Err.* III. i Who is that at the doore yᵗ keeps all this noise? **1622** BBE tr. *Aleman's Guzman d'Alf.* II. 42 It did mightily e me,..that I could not call vnto them to keepe lesse se. **1633** G. HERBERT *Temple, Redemption* 12 At length I rd a ragged noise and mirth Of theeves and murderers. **2** ROWE *Tamerl.* IV. i, Thou hast thy sexes Virtues, Their ectation, Pride, Ill Nature, Noise. **1775** tr. *Scarron's n. Rom.* I. 286 Zounds, sir, don't keep such a noise about r boots, but rather take mine, so you will but let us sleep. **4** DICKENS *Mart. Chuz.* xxv, I wish you'd hold your se! **1850** BROWNING *Bp. Blougram's Apol.* 19 When ner's done, And body gets its sop and holds its noise And es soul free a little.

b. ***without noise***, in a quiet manner; without y display, privately. *Obs.*

390 GOWER *Conf.* I. 100 Prively withoute noise He ngth this foule grete Coise To his Castell. **1560** DAUS tr. *dane's Comm.* 114b, She would be buried without any npe or noyse. **1614** RALEIGH *Hist. World* II. 508 After this e Ezechia had rest, and spending without noyse that ition which God had made unto his life. **1662** J. DAVIES *Olearius' Voy.* 110 They were married on Shrove-day..but without any noyse.

c. Strife, contention, quarrelling. *Obs.*

84 CAXTON *Fables of Æsop* II. xii. 48 Oftyme it happeth of a fewe wordes euyll fette, cometh a grete noyse and nger. **1491** —— *Vitas Patr.* (W. de W. 1495) I. cxix. /1 Neuer to haue noyse with a nother it is angels lyfe. **0** PALSGR. 248/1 Noyse, frayeng, *castille*.

, †**a.** Common talk, rumour, report; also, evil ort, slander, scandal. *Obs.*

297 R. GLOUC. (Rolls) 6383 He let caste þis traitour in þe ninge late At an fenestre in temese, noise vorto abate. **00** *Rom. Rose* 3971 To me it is gret hevinesse, That the se so fer is go, And the sclaundre of us two. **1426** *Paston* I. 26 To declare aught of this matier in stoppyng of the se that renneth in this case. **1461** *Ibid.* II. 50 Ther is gret se of this revell that was don in Suffolk be Yelverton and ey. **c1478** *Plumpton Corr.* (Camden) 38 The great ior, slaunder, & full noyse of your tenants..att they d be untrew peopell. **1523** LD. BERNERS *Froiss.* I. cccliv. The castell..the whiche the Gauntoyse hadde brente, he noyse ranne. **a1572** KNOX *Hist. Ref.* Wks. 1846 I. 92 noyse of the death of King James divulgat,..the hartes men begane to be disclossed. **1655** *Nicholas Papers* nden) II. 179 All agree in the noise of more... W. TEMPLE *Mem.* Wks. 1720 I... e magnificent Pre...

stelyng of shepe. **1470-85** MALORY *Arthur* VIII. vii. 282 By cause of that noyse and fame that thou hast. **1549-62** STERNHOLD & H. *Ps.* lxxxix. 16 Through thy righteousness have they a pleasant fame and noyce. **1556** *Aurelio & Isab.* (1608) N vj, Myn ill noise makes me worthey that all the wordes ill saide againste them be unto me attributede.

†**c.** Distinction, note. *Obs. rare*⁻¹.

1670 G. H. *Hist. Cardinals* II. III. 201 They were persons of no great noise, but resolute, modest, courteous.

d. An utterance, usu. in phr. ***to make noises***: to express (something) vocally; freq. with defining adj. prefixed.

1951 N. MARSH *Opening Night* vii. 152 Dr. Curtis said: 'I'd better go and make professional noises at him.' **1955** *Times* 21 July 8/6 If this is so, 'why then the noise about the 12 German divisions in W.E.U. and N.A.T.O.?' **1956** N. MARSH *Off with his Head* (1957) v. 91, I suppose I ought to make a polite noise. **1965** *N.Y. Times* 15 Sept. 42 Leftwing Liberals have made neutralist noises in the past. **1967** *New Scientist* 22 June 718 General Electric and Alcoa, for example, are making noises about getting into city building. **1969** S. HYLAND *Top Bloody Secret* iii. 232, I made the right kind of encouraging noises. **1971** *Guardian* 14 May 24/2 There is a temptation to see the hand of Tate and Lyle and Mr Cube in any political noises from the sugar trade. **1971** P. WORSTHORNE *Socialist Myth* iii. 32 The Labour Party cannot make the classical patriotic noises as convincingly as the Tories. **1973** *Times* 8 Jan. 3/3 Although the city council is, as they see it, making more friendly noises, its policies on development and road building..set it on a collision course.

3. a. A loud or harsh sound of any kind; a din.

c1290 *St. Barnabas* 51 in *S. Eng. Leg.* I. 28 Al þat on half daschte a-doun..of þis temple with gret noyse and soun. **13..** *E.E. Allit. P.* B. 849 þe god man glyfte with þat glam & gloped for noyse. **1390** GOWER *Conf.* III. 216 Many an other tente mo With gret noise, as me thoghte tho, It threw to grounde. **c1400** MAUNDEV. (Roxb.) xxxi. 138 þer es herd noyse as it ware of trumppes. **a1450** *Fysshynge w. Angle* (1883) 5 þe noyse of houndes & blastes of hornes. **a1533** LD. BERNERS *Huon* xxiii. 68 The water..made suche a noyse that it myght be herde .x. leges of. **a1548** HALL *Chron., Hen. VI* 95 By the noyes of a spanyell was on a night a man espied and taken. **1582** LICHEFIELD tr. *Castanheda's Conq. E. Ind.* 73b, The tackling.., with the great force of the winde, made such a terrible noyse, and was so fearefull to heare. **1624** QUARLES *Job* xvii 54 Who ever heard the voyce Of th' angry heavens, unfrighted at the noyse? **1653** tr. *Carmeni's Nissena* 124 By the noise of Trumpets and beating up of Drums. **1710** J. CLARKE tr. *Rohault's Nat. Philos.* (1729) I. 185 Gunpowder when it takes Fire in a Cannon..makes such a prodigious Noise. **a1774** GOLDSM. *Nat. Hist.* (1776) I. 160 This motion continued the remaining part of the day..; nor did the noise cease during the whole time. **1848** L. HUNT *Jar of Honey* ii. 23 A noise is heard like the coming of a thousand chariots. **1888** MISS BRADDON *Fatal Three* I. iv, I never heard any one make such a noise on a piano.

b. The aggregate of loud sounds arising in a busy community.

c1450 tr. *De Imitatione* I. xx. 25 þat he wiþdrawiþ him fer fro seculer noyce. **c1610** *Women Saints* (1886) 44 Ill brooking secular noise, and worldlie companie of the towne. **1651** HOBBES *Leviath.* I. ii. 5 Obscured and made weak; as the voyce of a man is in the noyse of the day. **1676** HALE *Contempl.* I. 286 In shady Privacy, free from the Noise And busles of the World. **1730** BERKELEY *Lett.* Wks. 1871 IV. 173 Preferring quiet and solitude to the noise of a great town. **1784** COWPER *Task* III. 379 A life all turbulence and noise may seem To him that leads it, wise. **1816** SHELLEY *Dæmon* I. 28 Seek far from noise and day some western cave.

c. ***noises off***: sound effects, usu. loud ... confused, produced off the stage ... by the audience ... Also ...

evaluating aircraft noise in terms of its intensity and duration.

1963 *Final Rep. Comm. Probl. Noise* 218 in *Parl. Papers 1962 3* (Cmnd. 2056) XXII. 657 During the Social Survey made in 1961 in the vicinity of London (Heathrow) Airport, measurement of noise levels and studies of the numbers of aircraft likely to be heard were made... The results have been combined..to form a Noise and Number Index (NNI). **1971** *Physics Bull.* Nov. 660/3 An exposure index for aircraft noise has been developed from this survey, called the noise and number index. This index is a combination of the average noise level measured at a point on the ground and the number of times a person is exposed to aircraft noise during a given period of time.

4. A sound which is not remarkably loud.

c1375 *Sc. Leg. Saints* xxvi. (*Nicholas*) 121 þane of þe noys of his fet he waknyt þane. **1387** TREVISA *Higden* (Rolls) III. 275 Democritus was woned to seie þat þe hestes of schrewes and þe noyse of þe wombe beeþ in oon place. **1560** DAUS tr. *Sleidane's Comm.* 232b, That noise..whan a man doeth rattle or shake together a number of dead mens bones. **1617** MORYSON *Itin.* I. 196 We tooke some rest,..but with such feare, as wee were ready to flie upon the least noise. **1642** FULLER *Holy & Prof. St.* I. xii. 36 Some report of sheep, that when they runne they are afraid of the noise of their own feet. **1697** DRYDEN *Virg. Georg.* IV. 801 A buzzing noise of Bees his Ears alarms. **1732** ARBUTHNOT *Rules Diet* in *Aliments*, etc. 315 A soft Noise of Water distilling by Drops into a Bason. **a1774** GOLDSM. *Nat. Hist.* (1776) VII. 28 The noise which the snail makes in moving the water. **1833** TENNYSON *Lady of Shalott* IV. iii, Thro' the noises of the night She floated down to Camelot. **1876** BRISTOWE *Th. & Pract. Med.* (1878) 364 The noises which attend the acts of coughing.

fig. **1660** SOUTH *Serm.* (1727) IV. 31 One would think, that every Letter was wrote with a Tear, every Word was the Noise of a breaking Heart.

5. a. An agreeable or melodious sound. Now *rare*.

?**a1366** CHAUCER *Rom. Rose* 79 Than doth the nyghtyngale hir myght To make noyse and syngen blythe. *Ibid.* 1416 The water, in renning, Gan make a noyse ful lyking. **c1403** LYDG. *Temple Glas* 1362 þe noise and heuenli melodie Which þat þei made in her armonye. **1500-20** DUNBAR *Poems* xlvi. 25 Nevir suetar noys wes hard with levand man, Na maid this merry gentill nychtingaill. **1535** COVERD. *Ps.* xlvi. 5 God is gone vp with a mery noyse. **a1553** UDALL *Royster D.* I. iv. 20 Up wyth some mery noyse, Sirs, to bring home the bride! **1585** T. WASHINGTON tr. *Nicholay's Voy.* III. ix. 84 Diuers cymbals..made a very plesant and delectable noyce. **1798** COLERIDGE *Anc. Mar.* 368 9 It ceased; yet still the sails made on A pleasant noise till noon, A noise like of a hidden brook.

†**b.** A company or band of musicians. *Obs.*

1558 in Nichols *Progr. Q. Eliz.* I. 39 Nere unto Fanchurch was erected a scaffolde richely furnished, whereon stode a noyes of instrumentes. **1594** LYLY *Moth. Bomb.* III. iv, Then I wish'd for a noyse Of crack-halter Boyes, On those hempen strings to be twanging. **1598** CHAPMAN *Blinde Beg. Alexandria* Plays 1873 I. 17 Oh that we had a noyse of musitions to play to this anticke as we goe. **1609** B. JONSON *Sil. Wom.* III. iii, The smell of the venison, going through the street, will inuite one noyse of fidlers, or other. **1636** R. GRIFFIN in *Ann. Dubrensia* (1877) 52 A Virgin-crew of matchlesse choyce,..attended with a noyse Of musique sweet. **1668** DRYDEN *Maiden Queen* III. i, I hear him coming, and a whole noise of fiddles at his heels.

transf. **1676** WYCHERLEY ... i, I cou'd as soon suffer a whole ... reat Man's Levee. ... (in other than ... outcry, to talk ... on Wks. 1720 II. ... 29) I. 300 For all ... is but little true ... /1 The French ... hey had gained. ... 9 Anatomists ... es of the same ... e object of ... (without ... on, esp. in ... of great ... that keeps ... Sir Walter ... App. V. 36 ... owe makes ... *War* Wks. ... mer that ... *s Disp. &* ... kes more ... *a* **1862** ... Black.. ... G. H. ... inning ... AMBERS ... h, she ... **1927** T. ... weekly ... ORTHY ... *ld of* ... the ... y iii. ... has ... EDY ... the

... *rolic like a* ... uch Powell, in his *Scouting* ... scouts in danger of detection to take ... and make a noise like a (say) thrush. ... in his ... haw-hawing chorus **1949** F. MACLEAN *Eastern* ... After some time had elapsed, there

7. In scientific use, a collective term (used without the indef. article) for fluctuations or disturbances (usu. irregular) which are not part

in the input circuit. **1932** F. E. TERMAN *Radio Engin.* vi. 207 The output currents obtained..in the absence of a signal voltage produce what is commonly referred to as 'noise' when flowing through a..loudspeaker, and it is also common practice to apply the term 'noise' to the corresponding radio-frequency currents obtained in the output of a radio-frequency amplifier, although these lie above the range of audible frequencies. **1940** ZWORYKIN & MORTON *Television* vi. 194 If the noise is appreciable compared with the picture signal, it appears in the reproduction as a myriad of constantly changing bright specks. **1953** J. B. CARROLL *Study of Language* vii. 201 It is ..necessary to study the effect of the signal-to-noise ratio on the efficiency of communication, noise being defined as that part of a received transmission which is extraneous to the original message. **1962** A. NISBETT *Technique Sound Studio* 262 In all electronic components and recording or transmission media the signal must compete with some degree of background noise. **1966** *New Scientist* 16 June 714/3 In this way a radar echo which may otherwise be hidden by 'noise' is rendered visible. **1968** J. LYONS *Introd. Theoretical Linguistics* ii. 88 The distortions produced in one's handwriting in a moving train can be attributed to 'noise'. **1970** O. DOPPING *Computers & Data Processing* i. 21 Information theory deals largely with what happens when a random interference ('noise') is superimposed on the desired signal. **1973** *Computers & Humanities* VII. 160 Knisbacher uses a generalized (context-free) grammar in his algorithm [for machine translation] but avoids the 'noise' of too many resultant analyses for each sentence by simulating context sensitivity within that context-free framework. **1974** *Nature* 10 May 192/1 As normally viewed, displays of video noise ('snow') have the appearance of fields of small speckles which seem to dart about at random.

8. *Comb.*, as ***noise abatement, control, level, -maker, -making, measurement, meter, pollution, reduction, suppression; noise-free, -measuring*** adjs.; **noise check** *Motor Rallying*, the use of a decibel metre to ensure that cars do not make too much noise; **noise contour**, an imaginary line or surface joining points where the noise level is the same; **noise factor** or **figure** *Electronics*, a quantity representing the additional noise introduced by a signal-processing device such as an amplifier (see quots.); **noise filter** *Electronics*, a filter for selectively reducing noise; **noise limiter** *Electronics*, a circuit or device for selectively reducing certain types of noise, esp. by momentarily reducing the output or the gain during peaks of greater amplitude than the desired signal; **noise-money** (see quot. 1883); **noise storm** *Astr.*, a radio emission from the sun consisting of a succession of short bursts or pips in the megahertz range that lasts for a period of hours or days and is associated with sunspots.

1923 *Health* II. 438 A real want, a very great want, and a very immediate want is a Noise-Abatement Society. **1973** *Scotsman* 13 Feb. 8/3 It would be very hard to sustain a reasonable argument against them on noise abatement grounds. **1960** S. TURNER *Rallying* vi. 68 One other sort of check which you must treat with respect is a noise check. **1963** [see *dust-raising* adj. (DUST *sb.*¹ 8 b)]. **1963** P. DRACKETT *Motor Rallying* iii. 37, I was remarkably unimpressed by the secrecy displayed by noise-check marshals on one big rally. **1971** *Physics Bull.* Nov. 656/1 During design studies of rotorcraft the noise of various designs is assessed by predicting an appropriate noise contour (usually 90 PN dB) and comparing it with the design noise target. **1973** *Times* 25 Apr. 19/6 If there were a prospect of drastically curtailing operations from Heathrow and Gatwick..before the time when the noise contours will start contracting through the increasing use of quieter aircraft, then there would be some point..in building Maplin. **1960** *McGraw-Hill Encycl. Sci. & Technol.* IX. 120/1 The first step in noise control is an analysis of the nature and extent of the problem. **1937** A. G. TYNAN in *Radio Engin.* July 21/2 Such a factor is very easily arrived at by multiplying the noise-signal ratio..by the sensitivity of the receiver in microvolts. This may be conveniently christened the noise factor. **1952** *Wireless World* June 224/1 There are various slightly different definitions of noise factor (in America, 'noise figure'). *Ibid.*, The noise factor is 3. It means that the result of amplifier noise is to make the noise 3 times as bad as in the ideal case where the signal source is the sole noise generator. *Ibid.*, In an ideal amplifier or receiver the noise factor..would be 1. **1962** *Rep. Comm. Broadcasting 1960* 333 in *Parl. Papers 1961 2* (Cmnd. 1753) IX. 259 The Band V tests have also shown that the noise factor of receivers in this Band is at present relatively high. **1944** *Proc. IRE* XXXII. 420/2 The noise figure *F* of the network is defined as the ratio of the available signal-to-noise ratio at the signal-to-generator terminals to the available signal-to-noise ratio at its output terminals. **1952** Noise figure [see *noise factor* above]. **1968** *Wireless World* Dec. 455/2 Noise figure = Total noise output power/Noise output power due to sources only. *Ibid.* 457/2 Negative feedback..has no effect whatever on the noise figure of an amplifier at any given frequency. *Ibid.* 458/2 A noise figure at 1,000 Hz of 0·02 dB. **1960** *McGraw-Hill Encycl. Sci. & Technol.* IX. 130/1 The tone control of ... as a noise filter, as when high-frequencies are cut down to reduce record noise. **1967** ... *Telemetry & Remote Control* ix. ... The characteristics of the noise filter are determined by ... system accuracy, and the allowable crosstalk between successive samples. **1934** ... practice in noise-free construction is now available for architects. **1966** D. G. ... *Metallogr.* 162 Careful design of ... scattered electrons yields ... **1925** *Sci. Amer.* June 422/3 ... static..what ... engineers ... in the disturbances in the ether. **1932** V. ... 257 The average street noise level in New York varies from about 47 to 80 db. **1959** ... be shown that helicopter operations can be carried out at a noise level tolerable to the ... *Down* xix. 111 Nowadays, among fields and woods, the noise level by day is..too high ... **1939** *Wireless World* 5 Jan. 15 (*heading*) Noise limiters suppressing interference in ... *Radio & Television Engineers' Ref. Bk.* xxxiii. 8 Noise limiters tend to be less efficient when ... extremely high selectivity. **1574** HOWSE in *Hist. Fam. Fortescue* (1869) II. 231 They found ... were gone back. **1610** ... Noyse money ... Of so much more ... *Gerardus* ... **1815** *Moore* ... 11/78 Among chatterers, drinkers, and all sorts of noise-makers. **1422** tr. *Secreta Secret., Priv. Priv.* 187 Thow shalt laugh wythout grynnynge, speke wyth-out cry or noyse-makynge. **1934** *Dorothy Dec.* 345 Efforts..are being made to provide standards of noise-measurement. *Ibid.* 347/1 The expert with his noise-measuring gear. **1964** R. F. FIELDS *Electr.*

Early in this century the Italian painter Luigi Russolo, who firmly believed that noise must be considered a legitimate part of musical vocabulary, built an orchestra of noise-making instruments to create an art that incorporated all of the sounds of Europe's industrialized soundscape.

[Italy, 1920s]

When glass is broken it tears at the heart like the sob of a woman.

R. MURRAY SCHAFER

The sound of the jackhammer is the archetypal noise of the city.

The U.S. Navy's Blue Angels make sound that rattles the bones, overloads the senses, and completely commands attention.

The industrial noise of the wrecking ball is a constant of city life. In order to create anew, the old has to be obliterated – Shiva dancing on concrete.

Demolition of the Athens Athletic Club, Oakland, California.

CHAPTER TWO

RHYTHMS OF WORK, WAR, AND PLAY

A festival enacts an ancient Japanese rice-planting ritual that is fast disappearing with the rise of mechanized agriculture. The *ta-bayashi* group consists of a leader (left top) who beats or rubs two pieces of bamboo together while he sings with the line of young women. They move backward through the field, transplanting rice seedlings into the paddies as they go. Rows of male drummers, gong players, and a flute player accompany the women. The rite is originally thought to have invoked the gods of sun and rain and thus insured the health of the year's crop. [Japan, ca.1980]

47

JUST WHAT DO WE FIND SO ATTRACTIVE ABOUT rhythmically controlled noise? Part of the answer is found in the nature of percussive noise. Loud! Sudden! It trips the switches in the oldest part of the brain, the part that quickly reacts with a fight-or-flight program, stimulating the release of adrenaline, the elixir of life; we never feel so alive as when the adrenaline is flowing. ❧ Part of the answer can be found in the midbrain, or mammalian brain, which is the part that assimilates all the rhythmic information captured by our senses. What the reptile brain processed as a series of potentially dangerous noises, the midbrain perceives as rhythm. "Hey, it's a rhythm," it says, "a powerful one, and the best thing to do with a powerful rhythm is entrain with it, beat with it." Which is exactly what the body, flooded with adrenaline but with nothing to flee from or fight, aches to do. It wants to move, to dance. ❧ This seems to account for the physiological pleasure of percussion. But there is also a higher level, the level of the cerebral cortex, the part of our brain that handles symbolic levels of meaning. What the rest of the brain hears as rhythm and noise, the cortex conceives in a larger majesty. ❧ The cortex recognizes this as particular noise, precise rhythm. It is the rhythm that has always been played in the village to mark particular points in time – to honor the gods, to celebrate community, to insure a good harvest, to commune with the larger pulse. ❧

Work

Before the Industrial Revolution work was often wedded to song, for the rhythms of labor were synchronized with the human breath cycle, or arose out of the habits of hands and feet.

R. MURRAY SCHAFER

Ten thousand years ago an agricultural revolution began to sweep the planet. Over time, large numbers of people ceased being hunters and gatherers and began learning the new rhythms of seeding and harvesting. One of the tools they used to adapt themselves to this novel use of the body was the drum. The drum made boring repetitive movement almost fun.

Even today you can find cultures where the hard labor of life is seldom attempted without the skillful application of rhythm and noise. When the Baule farmers of West Africa's Ivory Coast work in the fields with their hoes and pickaxes, they are accompanied by drum, xylophone, and other instruments playing rhythms perfectly suited to their movement and moment. The shepherd's bell, the carpenter's hammer also speak in rhythm.

Four smiths work together, rhythmically striking an anvil, each with his own pitched hammer. Musical notes are everywhere in this woodcut — under the window, on the far side of the doorway, on the anvil stand, on the smiths' hammers.

It's an allegory for the origins of music from the tuned hammers of the Bible's first musician, Jubal. [*In Tubalcain's Smithy*, title page of *Musicae Elementa*, by Martin Kromer, Cracow, Poland, 1532]

Rhythms of Work, War, and Play

49

Planet
Drum

If ten villagers are brought together to work without a musician, nothing will be accomplished. The group chooses a musician to play for them while they work. The productivity of the group depends on the musician who accompanies them. A salary increase could not be as effective. Whipping would only provoke revolt. A good musician behind the group, who follows the rhythm of each member, will help them all to accelerate. His playing will make the work enjoyable, or at least less painful.

YAYA DIALLO

In Arta, Greece, a prize goat is adorned with a *dhiplokypros* (cast bronze double bell). From the earliest times, herders have used bells to locate their flocks and to protect them from evil. Particularly elaborate bells are used in Greece; each has a slightly different sound, so individual animals can be found. [Ca. 1979]

Drum and xylophone join a harp in music to give rhythm to collective farming work.
[Baule people, Ivory Coast, 1965]

Communication

When the Europeans arrived in central and western Africa, they were astonished to discover that the people who lived there possessed a sophisticated communication system consisting of hollowed giant logs known as slit-gongs. Ingeniously positioned to take advantage of the natural acoustical properties of rivers and valleys, these gongs provided the people of the forest with a percussive telegraph system.

The bush telegraph is only one kind of African talking drum. More portable is the *dundun,* an hourglass-shaped, two-headed drum whose twin heads are laced together by thongs of gut or leather. By manipulating tension on these thongs, a player can alter the pitch of the tone he is making, thus enabling the *dundun* to "talk," or produce tones that sound like words. A master drummer can maintain a regular monologue on a talking drum, saying hi to different people, cracking jokes, telling proverbs.

A classic talking drum, the *dundun.* [Burkina Faso, 1966]

DRUM LANGUAGE

Another great obstacle to the relaying of drum messages over great distances is the fact of the tribal nature of most drum languages. Since the drum language is based on the tribal tongue it is usually understood only by members of the tribe. There is no "international" drum language in Africa any more than there is a common spoken language.... So that at the boundary of the tribal group sending out a message there would be a check in transmission. This check could only be overcome if a drummer were available who understood the drum language of his own and of the neighbouring tribe. Such men do occur in boundary villages. Children of parents who come from two different tribes often learn both languages and become bilingual on the drum. But they are not numerous and this fact makes it difficult to relay a drum message across the boundary of the tribe. Thus, many of the stories of news travelling across vast areas of Africa in a very short time must be accepted with great reserve even though the drum language may seem to provide an explanation.

J. F. CARRINGTON

The islanders have not yet adopted electric signals but possess, however, a system of communication quite as effective. Their huge drums by being struck in different parts convey language as clear to the initiated as vocal speech.

SIR HENRY M. STANLEY

A drum hut in central Africa houses a large slit gong carved from a log. The drummer exploits the natural sound-carrying ability of the waterway. [Lokele people, Zaire, 1940s]

DRUM HUT

*W*hen the anthropologist John Roscoe came to Banyankole, he found, at a little distance from the royal kraal, a small enclosure in which stood the hut of the royal drums. The hut was always domed and might have no point or pinnacle; inside there was a stand or bed on which lay two drums. At the back of the hut behind the bed lay a quantity of material for repairing these drums, and this had to be carefully guarded for it might not be used for any other purpose. To the left of the hut was a bag, in which were the instruments necessary for taking an augury should it be needed, and beside it lay some whistles and an iron rod upon which the tools for making the drums were sharpened, for this might not be done upon a stone. In front of the bed or stand was a row of milk pots belonging to the drums in which the daily offerings of milk were put. The chief drums were the two which lay upon the bed. These were covered with white skins with a black strip across them, making them look like a pair of great eyes in the gloom of the hut.

A sacred herd of cows yielded a supply of milk which was daily offered to these drums in the pots which stood in front of them. It was placed there in the morning and remained until nine or ten o'clock, by which time the drum-spirits had taken the essence and the remainder might be drunk by the guardians. There was also a woman, who was known as the "wife of the drums," and whose duty it was to look after the milk, the churning, and the covering of the drums. Another woman looked after the fire in the drum-house, which had always to be kept burning because the drum-spirits required warmth.

Offerings of cattle or beer were made to the drums by chiefs when a son had been born to them or when they had received promotion to some office or had been successful in some expedition and earned the commendation of the king. The king also made an annual offering of cows to the drums, so that they possessed a large herd; those offered to the first of them had to be red or white and those for the second black. These cows were sacred and the king alone might order one to be killed; no one but the guardians might eat the meat of an animal thus killed and the skin was kept for repairing the drums. It was from these cows that the milk was taken which was daily offered to the drums, and from the surplus milk butter was made for smearing on them.

CURT SACHS

Another kind of talking drum, the paired *atumpan* of the Akan people, is played by a master drummer. [Ghana, 1964] ▶

A village chief offers pieces of cooked chicken and rice with palm oil sauce to his ancestors, who were drummers. Many cultures believe that drums have resident spirits, ancestors or others who must be honored by offerings of food and drink. [Dan people, Ivory Coast, 1965] ▼

Planet Drum

54

What we have offered to you, drum, now it's cooked.
To all of you, gods, I offer you your chicken.
The chicken I spoke of, there it is, cooked.
Grant us good fortune!
Grant us wealth!
Grant us children!
Grant us good fortune!
The chicken we killed in your honor, there it is, cooked.

DAN VILLAGE CHIEF, IVORY COAST (1965)

Hortators

Beating the cadence on a large drum or slab of wood, the hortator held a unique position in the hierarchy of a ship's personnel. Boats powered by rowers cannot go anywhere without precisely coordinated rhythmic movement.

The hortator was a laborer, like the rowers, subject to the captain's commands. He got as much mileage out of the crew as possible without driving them to collapse. He knew their potential and limits. His sensitivity meant the difference between victory and defeat, life and death.

The African sculptor, perhaps wanting to show a European warship from a local perspective, carved this crew in German naval uniform paddling a Cameroon war canoe. The hortator is beating on a slit-gong. [Cameroon, early twentieth century]

"I can't stand his attitude."

In this re-creation of a Roman galley crew from around the time of Christ for the Hollywood film *Ben Hur,* men strain as the hortator's incessant beat drives them on, backed by the master's whip. [United States, 1927]

Early War

The drum beats. The adrenaline flows. And we either dance or we fight. Alongside the dance drum and the work drum, we have to set the war drum. Drums were the driving force behind the percussive din that characterized the ancient art of war. The name of the game was to energize your troops while terrifying your enemies with the thunderous noise you could make.

Mongol soldiers use kettledrums to exhort the troops and relay commands above the din of battle. [Painted illustration from *Jami 'at-tawarikh*, History of the World, by Rashid ad-Din, Persia, ca. 1306]

On the title page of the medieval *Spiezer Chronicles* by Diebold Schilling, a bear general rallies his bear troops for battle, while the band of fife and drum plays. [Switzerland, 1339]

Where drums beat, laws are silent.

ANONYMOUS PROVERB

At the battle of Actium (31 B.C.) it is said that Queen Cleopatra used numerous sistra, played by women, to intimidate the enemy, giving rise to the appellation "Cleopatra's war trumpet." It is difficult…to believe that the sound produced by a large body of women shaking such instruments could terrify a powerful foe.

JAMES BLADES

Kettledrums in a military parade, a conspicuous display of pomp and circumstance. [Engraving, England, ca. 1760]

In this massive mounted military band on parade are eight drums, six trumpet players, six cymbal players, and three players of pairs of kettledrums on camelback. Besides their military function, these noisy bands played for sporting events and ceremonies, whenever the clatter of officialdom needed to be heard. [*March of the Mehter*, from *Surname-i Vehbi*, Turkey, early 1700s]

SHAH-NAMA
THE EPIC OF KINGS

The commander of the Mazandarani army immediately issued the order that his troops as one man should lift up their heads and go into battle displaying the courage of tigers. Each man drew the sword of vengeance and the armies flung themselves upon each other. On either side resounded the trumpets and drums, the air became blue [with dust] and the ground black as ebony. Like the lightning that flashes from the midst of the dark cloud, so rays flickered from the battle-axe and sword. The air gleamed red, black and violet from the multitude of lances and the colours of the banners. At the shouts of the Divs and the noise made by the black dust rising, the thunder of drums and the neighing of war horses, the mountains were rent and the earth cleft asunder. So fierce a combat had been seen by no man before. Loud was the clash of the battle-axes and the clatter of swords and of arrows; the warrior's blood turned the plain into marsh, the earth trembled a sea of pitch whose waves were formed of swords, axes and arrows. Panting horses floated, like ships at sea, speeding onwards till they sank. Axes rained blows on helmets and skulls as fast as autumn gales blow down the leaves in showers from the willow-trees.

RECOUNTED BY ABU'L-QASIM FIRDAUSI (941–1019)

Animal soldiers with swords and halberds, off duty in the guardroom. Their snare drums, field drums, and colors lie on the floor while they pass the time. Abraham Teniers was making fun of his brother David's more serious work, a painting of virtually the same scene but with human characters. [Painting by Abraham Teniers, Flanders, seventeenth century]

The Battle of Blenheim is over (August 13, 1704) and the kettledrums lie discarded beside the banner of the losing side. An alliance led by the British Duke of Marlborough has just defeated the French and Bavarian forces, who were making their way toward Vienna with dreams of conquest. [Detail from *The Blenheim* tapestry, England, eighteenth century]

"Take my drum to England, hang et by the shore,
Strike et when your powder's runnin' low;
If the Dons sight Devon, I'll quit the port o' Heaven,
an' drum them up the Channel as we drummed them long ago."
Drake he's in his hammock till the great Armadas come,
(Capten, art tha sleepin' there below?),
Slung atween the round shot, listenin' for the drum,
An' dreamin' arl the time o' Plymouth Hoe.

SIR HENRY NEWBOLT

◄ Rembrandt's drawing features mounted African kettledrummers, likely seen by him in an Amsterdam pageant. As far back as 1085, the Moors had used African drummers in an attack upon Castile. The tradition of using blacks, costumed in exotic garb, as drummers in European military bands, continued until the mid-eighteenth century. [*Two Negro Drummers Mounted on Mules*, by Rembrandt van Rijn, Netherlands, ca. 1637]

As the poem tells it, great English seaman, Sir Francis Drake (1540–1596) asked his loyal crew to hang his drum at Plymouth, England; if it were ever beaten in time of danger, he promised to return. The drum waits to this day.

Rhythms of Work, War, and Play

61

Ranks of drummers at the rear control the rhythm of the battle, urging and exhorting British troops into combat against the Continental army at Bunker Hill during the American Revolution. [United States, 1898]

See, the conquering hero comes!
Sound the trumpet, beat the drums!

THOMAS MORELL

What was going on in Napoleon's mind after his defeat at the Battle of the Nations (Leipzig) in 1813? Head in hands, the general sits on an abandoned field drum and waits hopelessly, staring into the face of Death. Death sits upon a useless cannon, right foot on Napoleon's staff, left foot tapping a cannonball. Symbols of defeat abound: Napoleon's flags have fallen, his drums are silent, his guns are broken, his sword is in its sheath. [Cartoon by Thomas Rowlandson, England, nineteenth century]

The drum played an important role in maintaining the morale of General Washington's Continental army at its low point in the harsh winter of 1777–78 at Valley Forge. American drum manufacturer William F. Ludwig commissioned this oil painting in the twentieth century.

The black men who played these instruments were dressed in most elaborate uniforms, with gorgeous slashed tunics and high feathered turbans of great splendour. It was part of their business to perform all sorts of contortions and evolutions whilst playing their instruments. One writer says: "I have often heard old soldiers of that period talk of the antics these negroes were so fond of displaying while on the march, such as throwing up a bass drumstick into the air after the beat, and catching it with the other hand in time for the next; shaking the 'Jingling Johnnie' under their arms, over their heads, and even under their legs, and clashing the cymbals at every point they could reach."

HENRY GEORGE FARMER

By the late nineteenth century the British Coldstream Guards band had enthusiastically borrowed from Turkish Janissary music, adding two tambourines and a "jingling Johnny." Exotic costuming was typical. [Mezzotint, England, 1790]

A military band instrument, the Turkish crescent or "jingling Johnny," was adopted by Europeans in the 1700s. This example from Turkey is now at the Royal Military School of Music, Kneller Hall, Twickenham, England.

Matthew Brady (or a member of his staff) photographed this little drummer boy from the Union army in the 1860s. The curled fingers of his left hand show a perfect grip for the rudimental drummer of his day. Drummers had to maintain their balance and continue playing despite uneven terrain, rain, mud, snow, freezing cold, gunfire, and other difficult conditions.

The essential duo of fife and drum was central to the military music of the American Civil War. [United States, 1860s]

With drums and guns, and guns and drums
The enemy nearly slew thee.
My darling dear, you look so queer,
Oh Johnny, I hardly knew ye.

ANONYMOUS

Rhythms of Work, War, and Play

65

Drums pervaded everyday life in the military, from waking up to going to war. Thus it was a terrible indignity for a soldier in disgrace **to be drummed out of the service.** [United States, probably nineteenth century]

According to the stroke of the drum, the soldier shall go, just and even, with a gallant and sumptuous pace.

GARRARD

This outdoor drum ensemble rallies the people of Adrianople to defend the star and crescent flag during the Crimean War. [Turkey, 1876]

Farewell the neighing steed, and the shrill trump,
The spirit-stirring drum, the ear-piercing fife,
The royal banner, and all quality,
Pride, pomp, and circumstance of glorious war.

WILLIAM SHAKESPEARE

A twenty-man drum and bugle corps marches at the head of a military parade during a peaceful period in Mexican history. [*Drum Corps, Mexican Army*, by Frederic Remington, United States, ca. 1889]

"The Chinese army – trumpets sounding the assembly, with accompaniment of the bass drum." [From *Scientific American*, 1900]

Rhythms of Work, War, and Play

The Incas had an unusual way of celebrating their victories, one that involved a unique kind of drum. The following excerpt from a chronicle of Peru written around 1600 describes the Inca Sijuraca's triumphal entry into Cuzco, after quelling a rebellion at Andaguáilas.

The common people were to come first, crying in loud voices, "May so excellent a king live many years!" Following them, were to come the trumpets and drums, which were not to cease sounding except to let the voices of the people be heard, who, after the manner of criers, were to say the above words. After these, came two thousand soldiers drawn up in war formation, with their captains and the insignia of their office. They [the officers] were elaborately adorned; on their heads they wore very elaborate head-dresses and medals, with many plumes of various colours, and with great plates of gold upon their breasts and shoulders; the men wore silver ones which they got as spoils from the conquered. In the midst, at intervals, they bore six drums in human form, made from the skins of the [enemy] caciques and captains who had distinguished themselves in the battle. Their skins were peeled off while they were yet alive, and, filled with air, they represented their owners in a very lifelike fashion [and the victors] played upon their bellies with sticks out of contempt. Last of these, came the drum made from the Lord of Andaguáilas, whom they killed in the battle. To the sound of these drums marched four thousand more soldiers. Behind them were many captive caciques and captains. They were followed by still more soldiers, and then came six more drums like the first, and in the rear of the captives, came the [other] Lord of Andaguáilas whom they took prisoner in battle. He came naked, with his hands tied behind him, like the other captives, but he was placed on an unadorned litter, so that he might be ignominiously seen by all. Around his litter were six drums made of his relatives, with which sound was made. Next, came a troop of criers who ceaselessly told how the king treated those who rebelled against him, and others told of the actions of the people of Andaguáilas; and then the trumpets and drums made a great noise and clamour, which caused horror and fear [in the hearers]. Following this spectacle, came three thousand orejones, richly dressed, and adorned with a diversity of plumes. These kept singing . . . a song of victory relating the events of the battle, the spirit and valour of the conquering king. Behind them, came five hundred maidens, the daughters of the important Lords, very well dressed, with garlands of flowers upon their heads, with branches in their hands and small bells on their legs, singing and dancing in measure [in honor of] the prowess of the Inga. These were followed by many principal Lords, who went before the litter of the Inga, some picking up stones and bits of straw from the pathway, and others scattering flowers.

THE HUMAN DRUM

PERU ~ INCA PEOPLE

Modern War

As warfare grew more complex, the function of the drum changed. The drum absorbed some of the signaling duties formerly carried out by the trumpet, particularly among the infantry. By the sixteenth century, European armies had developed a codified set of drum rudiments (or standard pattern of beats) that allowed leaders to communicate various messages such as "advance" or "retreat" to their troops.

Drummers held a privileged position on the field of battle. It was considered dishonorable to strike or wound a drummer, though capturing a foe's drums was a glorious achievement. In fact, capturing a drum was the only way many regiments obtained some of the more valuable military drums.

The classic military drum was the snare drum because it offered the best balance between size and sound. Small enough to be carried by a single soldier — some of the bigger kettledrums had to be mounted on horseback or drawn in a carriage — it produced a sound that carried a long way, the snares vibrating against the underside of the drum to give it a bite that penetrated the thick noise of battle.

As the technology of war changed, the drum's usefulness on the battlefield diminished. The invention of the repeating rifle, for example, meant the end of the strategic "volley," which was regulated by the drum. Soldiers could now fire at will. With the advent of electronic communications in this century, the drum became all but obsolete as a tool of war. It is now an instrument of pomp and ceremony.

In some sense, the drum has reverted to its original use, that of energizing and uniting the troops. Modern armies continue to march to the beat of the drum, the throb of the membrane amplified by the percussive noise of thousands of marching feet. The rhythmic energy generated by marching not only stimulates the body but also forges within each soldier a sense of group unity, a feeling of entrainment with a larger organism.

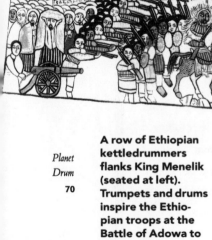

A row of Ethiopian kettledrummers flanks King Menelik (seated at left). Trumpets and drums inspire the Ethiopian troops at the Battle of Adowa to victory over the Italian invaders. The vicious battle included shooting, castration, decapitation, and other mutilation. The row of kettledrummers is directly descended in the tradition of the Ethiopian church from the drummers who announced the end of the world. [Ethiopia, ca. 1900]

We…encounter deliberate attempts to reproduce the apocalyptic noise throughout the history of warfare, from the clashing of shields and the beating of drums in ancient times right up to the Hiroshima and Nagasaki atom bombs of the second world war.

R. MURRAY SCHAFER

George Grosz depicts the horrors of Nazi Germany as a noisy phenomenon. A jackbooted foot, phonograph, and military drum compete for the crowd's attention while Hitler, shown with a party hat, holds a megaphone in one hand and a ratchet in the other, the ultimate master of sound. [*The Rabble-Rouser*, by George Grosz, Germany, ca. 1933]

I have become Death, the Destroyer of worlds.

J. ROBERT OPPENHEIMER, QUOTING *THE BHAGAVAD GITA*

"Priscilla," a 37-kiloton atomic bomb. [United States, 1957]

The drum is a power instrument, here adorned with the lightning symbols of the SS, representing the power to discipline. Hitler rode to power on the backs of the Hitler Youth. Their passion and dedication were aroused by the führer's powerful rites, extolling nationalism and discipline, and channeling their idealism to become part of the ever-powerful ritual of mass drumming. These fifteen-year-old children were the future soldiers for the armies of the Third Reich. [Germany, 1940s]

The orchestra of the Jewish ghetto in Korno. [Poland, ca. 1939]

One cannot hear the music well from Ka-Be. The beating of the big drums and the cymbals reaches us continuously and monotonously.... We all look at each other from our beds, because we all feel that this music is infernal.... When this music plays we know that our comrades, out in the fog, are marching like automatons; their souls are dead and the music drives them, like the wind drives dead leaves, and takes the place of their wills.

There is no longer any will: every beat of the drum becomes a step, a reflected contraction of exhausted muscles. The Germans have succeeded in this. They are ten thousand and they are a single grey machine; they are exactly determined; they do not think and they do not desire, they walk.

PRIMO LEVI

Play

In Africa they say there is no rhythm without its accompanying dance, that the rhythm of the dancing body complements the rhythm of the music, and to separate the two is to understand nothing.

Dancing allows us to lose ourselves in a larger communal pulse. In many traditional cultures, tribal cohesiveness is maintained through a calendar of ritual events in which the village frequently dances from dusk until dawn. But the need for a community to dance together is not just confined to traditional

In some countries, people gather around long instruments that require playing by many members of the community. A hollow log may serve as a communal drum. [Probably Salish or Haida people, Alert Bay, British Columbia]

The circus comes to town, bringing its own beat with it. [Chicago, 1943]

societies. We all need to celebrate life, our life together, whether in a unique, specialized moment like a wedding, or at a Friday night dance for teenagers, or at a carnival, or as a solitary street kid dancing down the block with his ghetto blaster under his arm.

For a culture to maintain its cohesiveness, it must have rhythms that everybody obeys, rhythms that are often buried so deep that our entrainment with them is for all practical purposes unconscious. To dance together becomes a symbolic affirmation of all the rhythms we share.

damn everything but the circus

e. e. cummings

OCEANIA

*The ultimate aim of dancing is to be able
to move without thinking, to be danced.*

JOHN BLACKING

**Women dance,
men play gongs.
Each dancer has
his or her own
unique way of** **realizing the movements, not follow-
ing a leader exactly
nor performing
choreographed
motions.** [Igorot
people, Philippines,
early 1900s]

Several men are seated in a special enclosure where four large slit-gongs are arranged in a square. A fifth, somewhat smaller instrument is placed at an angle to the others and its player directs the group. ['Are'Are people, Malaita, Solomon Islands, 1970]

Slit-drums…are believed to represent ancestral voices which encourage the living to dance into a state of communal ecstasy in order to banish personal preoccupations and bring those dancing into communion with collective forces passed on from the dead to the living and those still to come.

ADRIENNE L. KAEPPLER

Balinese musicians play an instrument of tuned bronze bars (*saron*) in a village orchestra known as a gamelan. [Bali, Indonesia, 1930s]

Dancers with elaborate facial paint perform for a festival audience, playing hourglass drums as they dance. [Papua New Guinea, 1978]

A young boy *kĕbyar* dancer performs squatting, coquettishly captivating his audience. *Kĕbyar* was a new style of dance and music developed in the 1930s and still popular today. Virtually every Balinese village has one or more gamelan ensembles to accompany its festive and communal events. [Bali, Indonesia, 1930s]

Two female *kundu* drummers of the Mendi people from the Southern Highlands Province, Papua New Guinea, wear opossum headbands adorned with feathers from parrots, hawks, birds of paradise, and eagles. They wear cone shells under their noses and as breastplates, and pearl shells for earrings. The drum on the right is covered with lizardskin, with pod rattles added to enrich the sound. The drum on the left is covered with snakeskin. [South Pacific Festival of the Arts at Townsville, Australia, 1988]

*Rhythms of
Work, War,
and Play*

A kabuki actor portrays a street musician who plays a *hatchōgane*, a rare instrument. The performer must whirl constantly to keep the set of small, tuned gongs up in playing position.
[Woodblock print, by Katsukawa Shunko, Japan, 1770]

An old Japanese man dances happily and plays a *kotsuzumi* (hourglass drum) after a hard day's work.
[Brush and ink painting, by Hokusai, Japan, nineteenth century]

Planet Drum

A young boy dances exuberantly to the music of a raucous folk ensemble that features a large hanging drum and a large hour-glass drum. [Korea, ca. 1800]

Ornately masked performers dance and drum in a street festival in rural Japan. [Hanamaki Festival, Morioka prefecture, Japan, ca. 1950]

An elaborate entertainment takes place at the court of the great emperor Akbar, who ruled India from 1556 to 1605. At right, an all-male *naubat* ensemble plays, with three men on pairs of kettledrums, one on cymbals, four on winds and brass. At lower left are two female dancers, accompanied by an all-female ensemble comprised of two frame drums, hand clapping, barrel drum, and small cymbals or clappers. [By Sānwala, from the *Akbārnama,* India, ca. 1590]

These near-legendary women dancers and drummers were so acrobatic that they were said to be able to shape their dance troupe so the audience would see an elephant. [Andhra Pradesh, India, ca. 1590]

Rattles made from cocoons and seedpods. Rattles made out of metal. Rattles attached to the ankles, the wrists, the waist, the neck. A rattle can extend the body's natural rhythms, and make music out of the dancing body. Rattles occupy a unique place in the audio spectrum. Their light tinkling and clinking hovers at the high end of the audible spectrum, like sparks thrown off by the dancer's energy.

Dancers can participate in music making in many ways, by clapping, stamping, body percussion, voice sounds, playing drums or other instruments during their dance, or by wearing bells, rattles, or sounding jewelry. [Nigeria, 1959]

The dancer's ankle bells serve as rhythmic accompaniment. [India, 1970s]

Tin cans with stones inside are worn as leg rattles. [Kenya, ca. 1932]

Even demons are moved to dance by the infectious rhythms of cymbals and clappers. [Painting from *The Fatih Album of Siyah Kalem*, Turkey]

At a wedding, a religiously derived performance of a *maulīd* (commemoration of a saint's death) with frame drums is presented. The use of similar drums has persisted for thousands of years in the Near East. [Dubai, United Arab Emirates, 1988]

Images of women dancing and playing tambourines abound in European graphic artists' visions of the Islamic world. Such romantic and exotic drawings became very popular in Europe at the end of the nineteenth century. This one, *Esmeralda*, came from an illustrated version of Victor Hugo's novel, *The Hunchback of Notre Dame*, published in France in 1831.

In Nile regions the sacred drums are hung in front of the chief's house or under the sacred tree of the village. When in front of the chief's house, they become identified with the mysterious power of his office. The drum is regarded as the mouthpiece of the god or spirit.

CURT SACHS

A traditional dance is performed with *tabl* (drum) accompaniment. [Khor Fakkan Society for Folk Arts and Theater, United Arab Emirates, 1988]

Bedecked with jewelry, a young girl dances to the rhythm of many clapping hands. Her people, Orthodox Muslims, fled Arabia in the middle of the nineteenth century after a dispute with other clans. [Rashaïda people, Ethiopian/Sudanese border region, 1980s]

The caption below this engraving in a London newspaper, dated May 27, 1896, reads: "The procession of the Mahmal takes place on the departure of the pilgrims' caravan from Cairo to Mecca. The Mahmal is a square wooden frame with a pyramidal top, covered with red cloth and richly embroidered with gold. Headed by a detachment of cavalry and infantry, it is followed by numerous dervishes, some bearing banners, some beating kettledrums, frame drums and barrel drums."

Three men play side drums, while others dance and play double-ended spoon pairs. Looking on is an international audience, including French soldiers, European gentlemen, and veiled local women. [Algiers, Morocco, ca. 1865]

Rhythms of Work, War, and Play

The predominant sound we heard as we developed in the womb was our mothers' heartbeats.... Is it any wonder that the reproduction of these pulsations alters our consciousness and heightens our awareness? Or reminds us what we already knew and have forgotten?

A. MANDALA

These women dancing, drumming, shaking, and rattling all have babies on their backs. Participation in communal rhythmic celebration begins at birth, or even before. [Senufo people, Ivory Coast, 1971]

For people of my tribe, with its rich musical context, exposure to music begins in the womb, when pregnant mothers join in the community dances. From inside the womb, our babies feel the vibrations of the rhythms enter their bodies. Infants are then wrapped onto their mothers' backs with a cloth and taken into the dancing circle with everyone else.

YAYA DIALLO

Dagomba boy.
[Ghana, 1970]

Pedestal drums are played en masse to accompany a spectacular leaping dance in the central African state of Rwanda. In the past drums were emblems of royalty, their sound representing the power of kings. [Ntere dancers, Tutsi people, Rwanda, 1950s]

These dramatic trapezoidal wooden slit-gongs are made from huge solid logs hollowed out through narrow, deep slits at the center. The enormous bass sound resounds over a broad area. [Ndengese people, Zaire, 1950]

Mock combats and stick dances are widespread. In a percussive *donga* stick combat, young men from rival tribes fight. The winner will enjoy tremendous honor and prestige. The only rule is that one may not kill one's opponent. [Surma and Mursi peoples, Ethiopia, 1980s]

The balafon is a portable marimba, a type of instrument widespread in West Africa. The marimba is comprised of a series of tuned wooden bars, their tones usually reinforced by gourd resonators under each bar. Instruments like these spread to the New World with the slave trade. [Senufo people, Ivory Coast, 1971]

Rhythms of Work, War, and Play

Dancers and drummer wear ankle rattles made from dried palm leaves folded in three with a pebble or seed inside each.
[Miango people, Nigeria, 1959]

In Cameroon, heavy paired bells provide the key rhythmic pattern for a genre of songs called "music for the hanging of a minister." [Bamun, Cameroon, 1960s]

Xylophones with gourd resonators are accompanied by drums. [Pende people, Zaire, 1971]

The drummer's eyes reveal the joy and intensity of complex rhythmic synchrony as he concentrates completely on the movements of the dancer. [Senegal, twentieth century]

Led by a deformed dwarf drummer and a fife player, troops march into a village and are welcomed by some local inhabitants while others point and laugh. [*The Moon Man of Sankt Schütze,* by Wilhelm Jury, Germany, ca. 1800]

A satirical engraving depicts a Frenchman draped from head to toe in musical instruments. [By Nicolas de Larmessin, France, seventeenth century]

Three children enjoy homemade music, the fiddler accompanied by friction drum and a gong improvised from a metal helmet struck with spoons. [*Two Boys and a Girl Making Music*, by Jan Molenaer, Netherlands, 1629]

Owl-masked drummers march in a D'Muggetätscher (Shrovetide or carnival association) festival in Basel. [Switzerland, 1960]

▲ A snare and a tenor drum join the high-pitched fife's melody in a folk version of the military grouping. [Barbados, 1986]

A street musician in the Caribbean shakes hammered tin rattles or maracas while blowing a police whistle. The whistle-blower is often the group leader, encouraging the other players with it and signaling changes from one rhythmic pattern to the next.

Actors sing and shake rattles as they rehearse a folkloric play. [Paramaribo, Surinam, 1980]

▲ A large shallow drum played simultaneously by a group of men seated in a circle around it provides the rhythmic foundation for many dances of the woodland American Indian tribes. [Ojibwa people, Wisconsin, 1916]

The buffalo-masked dance by people from the Acoma Pueblo is said to have been adopted through trade or other contact with a Plains Indian tribe. [New Mexico, ca. 1940]

Capoeira

Capoeira is a Brazilian martial art, dance, and spiritual discipline that was brought to Brazil five hundred years ago from Angola. In Brazil today, capoeira schools are widespread, particularly in the state of Bahía.

The musical bow berimbau leads dancers from one sequence of actions to another. Participants must be in top condition to meet the demands of this strenuous art. In the streets it can be used in self-defense, but during practice no physical contact should be made.

Written references to capoeira date back more than two hundred years. One story has it that black slaves were the first capoeiristas, developing a homegrown martial art to the accompaniment of musical bow. Not allowed to carry weapons on pain of death, they were readying their bare hands and feet for escape. The bow player also served as lookout, and when he saw a plantation guard coming, changed the pattern. Then the fighters would change their movements to happy dancing, and the guards would pass by unconcerned.

AIRTO MOREIRA

Sketches of *capoeira* by Carybé. [Brazil, twentieth century]

As many as seventy singers and two hundred dancers may perform the intricate songs, elaborate circlings, and interweavings of the great corn dances. Corn dances are associated with agricultural festivities, especially at harvest time. They are performed in lines. The rattles the dancers use are generally large gourds filled with dried seeds, pebbles, or even buckshot. [Tewa people, New Mexico, early twentieth century] ▼

This early representation depicts an Aztec festival ensemble, with *huehuetl*, *teponaztli*, rattle, and plumes. [Mexico, seventeenth century]

Besides developing co-operation, communal dancing may also encourage restraint and the ability to attend to a single task, which are unique capacities of man amongst primates.

JOHN BLACKING

CHAPTER THREE

RHYTHMS OF LIFE AND DEATH

At the "Whirling Dervishes" annual gathering, a ritual of an Islamic mystical order is reenacted. This Sufi performance draws thousands of tourists. The dancers are said to experience themselves in essential unity with the divine spirit. [Konya, Turkey, 1970s]

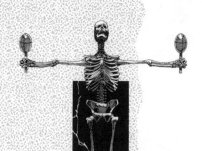

HOSE CULTURES THAT CHOOSE TO ACCESS THE
higher domains – the spirit world, the other world, heaven,
Valhalla, transpersonal consciousness, the collective unconscious,
name it however you prefer – have often used some form of rhythmically controlled noise to facilitate the communion. ॐ Shamans
say they "ride their drum" to the World Tree. The classic possession cultures say that the *Orisha,* the ancestor spirits, ride the
rhythm of the drum down into the dancing bodies. Work drum,
dance drum, war drum, *trance* drum. ॐ How does rhythmic
music serve as a catalyst for transformation? What role does the
musician play? How much training is required before a drummer
can handle these powerful trance rhythms and not become
entranced? What quality of balance is needed before we can
dance at the edge of magic and not slip? ॐ ॐ ॐ ॐ ॐ ॐ ॐ ॐ

Bacchanal

To dance is to take part in the cosmic control of the world. Every sacred Dionysian dance is an imitation of the divine dance.

HAVELOCK ELLIS

Ecstatic dancing and drumming flourished with the Neolithic mother goddess cultures from 9000 to 4000 B.C. The crumbling of this sophisticated culture in the millennium before the rise of Sumer is one of the ancient world's great untold stories.

Remnants of their old earth-based religion persisted into ancient times, showing up most vividly in the cult of Dionysus, which flourished in the centuries immediately preceding the birth of Christ. Most of the descriptions we have of this cult come from its detractors, who depict it as a drunken revelry in which wildly dancing men and women sought *ekstasis* — the Greek word for ecstasy.

From ancient Greece until today, artists have been inspired to illustrate the divine madness of the Dionysian (or Bacchanalian) cults. Over time, elements of older fertility rites, sacrificing and giving thanks to the mother goddess, were combined with seasonal celebrations of sowing and harvest. Eventually the goddess was forgotten, yet women still controlled the rhythm of the rituals with frame drums and tambourines. Besides the musical instruments, common elements include wine jugs, grapes, leopard skins, and the dance of celebrants in ecstatic and sensual abandon.

We recognize the classic woman-with-tambourine in this modern drawing. [*Dancer with Tambourine*, by Pablo Picasso, 1938]

Bacchante. [By William Etty, England, ca. 1825]

Creating the rhythms for this orgiastic dancing was a percussive orchestra made up of clappers, cymbals, tambourines, frame drums, and the eerie drone of the double-piped *aulos*.

In Rome, Dionysus's counterpart was the god of wine, Bacchus, and the ecstatic group rituals were called Bacchanalia. Entrancement in the revel is induced by music and heightened by wine. As Christianity came to dominate, during the reign of Constantine (288–337 A.D.), virtually all vestiges of the old rituals were eliminated, though a faint echo can still be found in the celebration of *carnaval*.

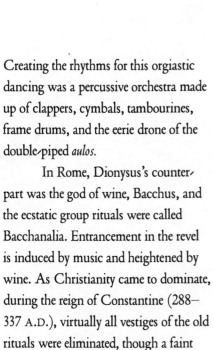

Dance of the Bacchantes.
[By Johann J. F. Langenhoeffel, Europe, 1798]

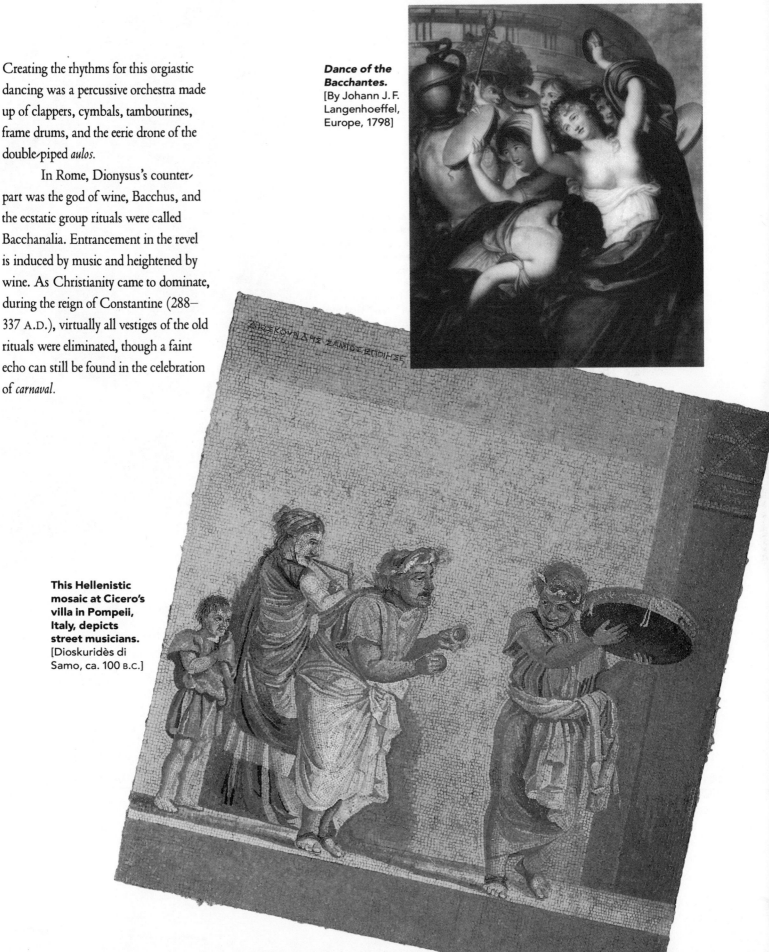

This Hellenistic mosaic at Cicero's villa in Pompeii, Italy, depicts street musicians.
[Dioskuridès di Samo, ca. 100 B.C.]

Psalms and Revelations

As we move deeper into the Christian era, the type of rhythmic affirmation represented by the Bacchanal almost disappears. Stillness rather than movement becomes the pathway to the spirit world. Contemplation and *agape* (the Greek word meaning a kind of selfless love) become the ideal. Most musical instruments are banned from the sanctuary, while continuing to appear in sacred art. The human voice, particularly the male voice, becomes the vehicle for worship; huge choruses assemble in the sacred space of stone cathedrals to chant the holy chants.

King David sits amid musicians and dancers, holding a harp, while the musicians around his throne "make a joyful noise unto the Lord," shaking crotals and dancing with abandon.
[Psalter, 872–920 A.D.]

Two angels exalt the Lord, one beating upon small kettle-drums and the other on a triangle, on this bronze door panel from the portal of the Oratorio di San Bernardino in Perugia, Italy. [By Agostino di Duccio, 1457–61]

Hallelujah.
Praise God in His sanctuary;
Praise Him in the firmament of His power.
Praise Him for His mighty acts;
Praise Him according to His abundant greatness.
Praise Him with the blast of the horn;
Praise Him with the psaltery and harp.
Praise Him with the timbrel and dance;
Praise Him with stringed instruments and the pipe.
Praise Him with the loud-sounding cymbals;
Praise Him with the clanging cymbals.
Let every thing that hath breath praise the Lord.
Hallelujah.

PSALM 150

The dances of creation and destruction merge in this image of Christ's nativity and the Last Judgment. The baby Jesus rings a pellet bell with each hand. His gaze locks with that of an angel playing similar bells, who seems to be the conductor of the heavenly orchestra. [Painting by Geertgen tot Sint Jans, Netherlands, late fifteenth century]

In this painting that hangs in the Vatican, an angel drummer plays upon a double-headed drum with a gut snare stretched across the top head. [Detail of fresco, by Melozzo da Forli, Italy, fifteenth century]

The twelve ringers stand ready to sound a peal, during the blessing of the new bells of St. Paul's Cathedral in London, November 9, 1878.

In the early centuries of the Christian church, the semantron or "holy board" was used to summon the faithful to prayer. It was quieter than a bell and was said to remind Christians of the sound of nails being driven through the limbs of their crucified Lord. [Great Lavra Monastery, Mount Athos, Greece, ca. 1972]

Masked Dance

The mask transforms. It is an image of the ability to communicate with the spirit world. Ancestor spirit, legendary hero, god and goddess, mythic creatures — donning a mask can call them all into being. It is said that you can release tremendous and mysterious power by simply joining a mask and a drum. This is a novel idea in our culture, where the use of masks is confined to such ritual occasions as Halloween, Mardi Gras, and the increasingly rare tradition of the costume party.

When the kachina mask is donned by a performer who understands the ceremony, personal identity is lost and the performer becomes an ancestor. [Hopi people, Shungopavi, Arizona, 1901]

A masked member of the men's secret society drums at the edge of the sacred forest. [Senufo people, Ivory Coast, mid-1960s]

Semesi masks, used in male initiation rites, help establish a channel to the spirit realm. [Papua New Guinea, ca. 1930]

I am certain that the use of the mask in the kachina ceremony has more than just an aesthetic purpose. I feel that what happens to a man when he is a performer is that if he understands the essence of the kachina, when he dons the mask he loses his identity and actually becomes what he is representing....The spiritual fulfillment of a man depends on how he is able to project himself into the spiritual world as he performs.

SAM GILL

The Dance of Death

Death is the ultimate edge – it dances with each of us. Following birth, it is life's second great transformation. The Tibetans use human bones and skulls in their rituals to remind them that one day we will be the skeletons that others are using for drums and drinking cups.

The closest that we in the West come to this is the European folk custom of wearing a *memento mori* – a reminder of death, usually a small skull carving on a necklace or ring. In the Middle Ages, however, the popular folk motif called the Dance of Death featured an orchestra of skeletons playing drums, xylophones, brass, and flutes. Some scholars think that the motif might have been inspired by the wholesale death caused by the bubonic plague. Whatever the cause, this imagery recalls a moment when the Christian world recognized and reacted to death's playful aspect.

Skeletons dance in a church graveyard. With a bone stick, the drummer beats a gut-snared drum. [*Heidelberger Totentanz, Germany, 1485*]

One skeleton plays a xylophone while another squires the old woman on her way. [*Old Woman,* by Hans Holbein the Younger, Germany, sixteenth century]

The conquest of the fear of death is the recovery of life's joy…. Life in its becoming is always shedding death, and on the point of death. The conquest of fear yields the courage of life. That is the cardinal initiation of every heroic adventure — fearlessness and achievement.

JOSEPH CAMPBELL

A noble couple is drummed off by a tabor suspended from the skeleton's waist. [*Noblewoman*, by Hans Holbein the Younger, Germany, sixteenth century]

A drumming skeleton, probably part of a larger ensemble for the festival *El Día de los Muertos* (Day of the Dead). [Mexico, late twentieth century]

Featuring an exuberant kettle-drummer, this Last Judgment scene abounds in noise, with blaring trumpets, trombone, hurdy-gurdy, and other outdoor instruments. [*End of Mankind*, by Hans Holbein the Younger, Germany, sixteenth century]

A skeleton on the old town clock in Prague rings a bell to mark the passing hours. [Czechoslovakia, 1990]

Rite and ceremony as well as legend bound the living and the dead in a common partnership.

JOHN DEWEY

Totentanz (Dance of Death) is painted on the dome of the charnel house at the Cathedral of St. George in Freiburg im Breisgau, Germany. [1723] ▼

A bell-ringing skeleton horseman leads a charnel cart. On the cart another skeleton plays a hurdy-gurdy. [Detail of *The Triumph of Death*, by Pieter Bruegel the Elder, Flemish, ca. 1562]

The women in this watercolor do not seem frightened of Death, but accepting. The mustachioed skeleton at left plays pipe and tabor. [By A. Kauw, probably Switzerland, 1649]

Skeletons play upon skeleton drums, one on a *taiko* (small barrel drum), the other a *da-daiko* (large barrel drum). A skeletal singer adds a skeletal melody. [Japan, nineteenth century]

The Tibetan Book of the Dead *speaks of apocalyptic sounds in the transition to the other side. Shortly after death, if liberation is not immediately achieved, we are said to glimpse a bright and radiant light, the light of our own essential nature. Issuing from that light is the "natural sound of Reality, reverberating like a thousand thunders simultaneously sounding." We are cautioned not to fear this sound or be in awe of it. Later, if our consciousness has not yet reached enlightenment, we will meet up with dancing beings representing knowledge, playing drums, bone trumpets, and skull tambourines. We hear a "frightful tumult… mountains crumbling down filling all the regions of the universe so that they rock and tremble and shake."*

D. A. SONNEBORN

One skeleton holds a fly whisk, the other a skull-tipped scepter. The dancing skeletons are both menacing and comical, characters from one of the religious tales annually enacted at Tibetan monasteries in the ritual dance drama of *'Cham,* traditionally accompanied by instruments including drums and cymbals. [*Lords of the Cemetery,* Tibet, probably twentieth century]

Around the corpse at a funeral, people dance and play percussion instruments, including a small drum, a large drum, a metal scraper, a calabash rattle, and a musical bow. [Senufo people, Ivory Coast, 1965]

Trance

Transformation — it's not necessarily cosmic or otherworldly. It can happen very naturally. It's a matter of attention. Remember disappearing into the buzz of a summer day as a child? Or lying on a riverbank watching the rippling flow of the current as the water slips downstream, carrying time with it? Or dancing effortlessly all night to a local garage band when you were sixteen?

Scholars speak of a spectrum of transformation with trance and ecstasy at opposite ends.

Trance is usually achieved at communal rituals, with plenty of loud music and dancing. The specifics — the costumes, music, and dance — vary from culture to culture, but the pattern underneath is identical: loud music and vigorous dancing lead to a state of overstimulation that can produce a form of egolessness that is the ground for any sacred exploration.

The second path, ecstasy, relies on contemplative solitude to bring about the required loss of self-consciousness. You sit quietly, slowly allowing your complex sensory apparati to shut down until everything fades away including yourself.

What's common to both trance and ecstasy, and to all the techniques in between, is a necessary and disciplined focusing of attention. All extraneous rhythms must be put aside to allow the celebrants to focus maximum energy on maintaining, at this time and place, this one rhythm, maintaining it until and through the point of transformation.

The Day of Treading was an annual ritual of an Egyptian Sufi order. The entranced dervishes lay face down and their sheikh rode over them on horseback to the sound of beating drums. Those whose bones broke under the hooves were assumed to have been weak in faith. [Cairo, ca. 1868]

Dervish dancers in northern India are accompanied by musicians playing two frame drums and a flute. Several dancers have become so strongly entranced that they have lost awareness of their bodies and are tended by novices from their order. [By anonymous Mughāl period artist, India, early seventeenth century]

*There is a small meal before daybreak
during Ramadan. It's called* sahur,
and traditionally, a drum-call announces it.

*Midnight. A man sits beside the gate to an empty courthouse,
drumming steadily the* sahur *drumbeat.*

Someone comes by. "Wait a minute! In the first place,
sahur *happens at dawn, or just before.
Midnight is no time for this noise.
And secondly there's no one around!
Why beat a drum if no ears will hear?
Is there some hidden intelligence in what you're doing?"*

The midnight sahur *drummer answers:*

*"Some people go to war.
Some endure painful difficulties.
Some wait patiently. Everybody does
service of some sort. Mine is drumming
at this gate where the only listener is God."*

JELALUDDIN RUMI

In fulfillment of a
sacred vow, this man
is walking three
miles carrying a
heavy yoke. His
flesh is pierced both
back and front with
108 hooks. He is
accompanied all
the way by the
beating of a drum.
[Singapore, 1932] ▼

The veiled dancer
reaches out to
touch the *tabl*. The
drum is considered
to have healing
power in the con-
text of this dance.
[*Khammari* dance,
Fatimah Shahhad
Musical Ensemble,
Doha, Qatar, 1988] ▼

Balinese villagers in trance turn their daggers on themselves under the power of the malevolent Rangda, a masked witch who uses her magic to deflect their aggression. The dancers fall to the ground until Barong, a friendly, lionlike creature, comes and sprinkles water to revive them. [Bali, Indonesia, 1937]

When the Indian yogi attains a state of liberation from the senses, he hears the anahata, the "unstruck" sound. Then perfection is achieved. The secret hieroglyph of the universe is revealed. Number becomes audible and flows down, filling the receiver with tones and light.

R. MURRAY SCHAFER

From the still center of his being, focused and silent, a Japanese Buddhist monk strikes a giant barrel drum at the Myorenji Temple in Kyoto. Stillness and motion are one and the same, as are sound and silence, self and drum. [Japan, 1984]

Stillness

It has always been the business of the great seers (known to India as "rishis," in biblical terms as "prophets," to primitive folks as "shamans," and in our own day as "poets" and "artists") to perform the work of…mythology by recognizing through the veil of nature, as viewed in the science of their times, the radiance, terrible yet gentle, of the dark, unspeakable light beyond, and through their words and images to reveal the sense of the vast silence that is the ground of us and all beings. Gods that are dead are simply those that no longer speak to the moral order of the day.

JOSEPH CAMPBELL

Monks play drums and cymbals in this procession at the Khampagar Monastery. [India, 1974]

Buddhist lamas chant during a dance ceremony.
[Sikkim, 1971]

All final spiritual reference is to the silence beyond sound. The word made flesh is the first sound. Beyond that sound is the great transcendent unknown, the unknowable. It can be spoken of as the great silence, or as the void, or as the transcendent absolute.

JOSEPH CAMPBELL

A Buddhist monk, Shinglay Lama, plays a double-headed drum held by a long handle.
[Sikkim, 1971]

Shaman's Drum

Shaman. The word comes from the pastoral herding peoples of the Asian steppes, who use it to refer to those individuals in a tribe or community who are professional trance-travelers, handling the tribe's communication between this world and the spirit world. Shamans are healers, psychics, weatherworkers; they lobby the higher powers to assure a good hunt. In modern psychological terms,

Blacksmith and shaman are from the same nest," says a Yakut proverb. At the beginning, the blacksmith has only his fingers, but he heals, predicts the future, and starting at the ninth generation, he embraces the art of sorcery and forges the metal ornaments for the shaman's costume.

ANDRÉ SCHAEFFNER

Tulayev, a Karagas (Soyot) shaman. [Irkutsk, Siberia, ca. 1927]

I am fighting for you to cure you.
I will suck out what is hurting you, to cure you.
The things I shall take out are the things that are
      causing your sickness.
Now I take Mother-bear and put her under my arm
As I get ready to look in the crystal, and
      I will help you.
Help us all.
Thank you.

SANTO DOMINGO
PUEBLO SHAMAN (1930s)

Central Asian and Siberian shamans take their journey to the spirit world to learn from the spirits how to cure an ailing individual or how to deal with communal problems. [Kamchatka district, Siberia, ca. 1840]

Planet Drum
126

you could say they have mastered such nonordinary states of consciousness as lucid dreaming, clairvoyance, clairsentience, and out-of-body travel. They are also actors and actresses, dancing on the edge in full view of their community, their transformation a public performance.

You don't just become a shaman. An initiation is required; a teacher is usually vital. The training is rigorous, often, in the classic shamanic cultures, to the point of near death. It is thought necessary to weaken the body almost to the point of extinction for the spirit world to establish a strong channel. Only after the spirits come, can a shaman leave his body and go adventuring up and down the World Tree. (The World Tree is the image the shamanic cultures give to the domain of experience that the occult tradition calls the Other World, and that some scientists of consciousness call the domain of nonordinary and transpersonal experience.)

A shaman typically needs three things: power songs to summon his spirit allies, spirit allies to guide him to the World Tree, and a drum to ride there on.

Nepalese shamans gathered to dance at dawn, beating their drums with anthropomorphically carved sticks. [Nepal, date unknown]

DAMARU

*B*efore Buddhists came to Tibet, there were powerful shamans, a religion called Bon, which still exists in some areas. The practitioners of Bon have legends of drums coming from the gods, flying through the sky with drums, and so on. The Buddhists wanted to distinguish themselves from these shamans, and so they did their rituals without drums.

Later, a great teacher, Tsong Khapa, had a friend named Chumbu Neljar, who did many rituals for the god Mahakala, and he used the drum damaru. Mahakala would come down and rumble around; sometimes during the ritual, if Chumbu was tired, Mahakala himself would play the drum. Tsong Khapa asked Chumbu, "Why do you use this drum? You know we don't use drums because that's the way of shamans." Chumbu replied, "I do it for Mahakala. He likes it."

Tsong Khapa was not convinced. He said, "Try not using it for a while, and see whether there's any difference. Personally, I think it's a superstition, and you don't really need it."

So Chumbu stopped using the damaru. But he felt unhappy, and never saw a trace of Mahakala. Everybody was miserable. When Tsong Khapa returned he asked, "Was there a difference?"

Chumbu replied, "There was a great difference! Mahakala didn't like it, and I don't like it. So please, let's go back to using the drum again."

Tsong Khapa then reinstituted the use of drums in ritual. They've been used ever since, and remain close to the heart of Mahakala and many other deities. Mahakala carries a skull damaru himself. The skull is a symbol of the unity of Emptiness and Great Bliss: inside, colored blood red, symbolizes Great Bliss; outside, colored white, symbolizes Emptiness. It is also a person turned inside-out, so to speak — their skull becomes a vessel of their realization of Emptiness and Great Bliss. The rattling of the damaru impels the hearer to dissolve their consciousness out of the coarse body of blood and limbs and flesh, and flow into their central nervous system, dissolving through inner heat into the inner channels and merging into realization of what is called "Clear Light" or "Translucent Light." When you do these practices, and when you are initiated, you must have a damaru, and must always keep it with you.

TARTHANG TULKU

Shattered burial platform of a Yakut shaman, his drum hanging on an adjacent tree. [Siberia, nineteenth century]

The Yakut shaman prefers, for the frame of his drum, wood from a tree that has been struck by lightning.

ANDRÉ SCHAEFFNER

His body deep in trance, the shaman is performing a healing ritual. His spirit is on a "magical flight," doing battle with spirits to diagnose and cure his patient's disease. Others keep the drumbeat going so he can find his way. [Nepal, 1976]

The most sacred of American Indian rituals are rarely photographed. This is a re-creation of one man's participation in a peyote ceremony. The drumming and song that has developed in peyote ceremonies is practiced by all celebrants in turn. [1927]

Shaman's Rattle

At a *zar* (a spirit possession healing) ritual, one performer wears a *manjur* (goat-hooves rattle belt) and shakes an *ashukhshaykhah* (tin-can rattle).
[Cairo, 1989]

The rattle is old, so old that it's normally counted, alongside concussion sticks and scrapers, as one of our first musical instruments, long antedating the drum. Take some pebbles, wrap a leaf around them, shake them well – you've created a rattle. Made out of seedpods, hollowed-out fruits, grass, leaves, fish scales, and all manner of shells, rattles represent an ingenious use of a local ecosystem's natural resources.

The rattle is the shaman's other tool of choice. The technology is so simple, yet the aural payoff is emotionally complex. Shake a rattle and you hear the rustle of brush outside the fire circle, or the scrape of branches in the wind, or the dry warning cough of the rattlesnake. Its distinctive voice, full of high frequencies, is said to serve as a focusing device.

In New Guinea, the history of rattles is also the history of river travel. Shells from all the various ecosystems are widely dispersed, suggesting that they were a prominent trading item. Only someone initiated into the subtle power of the rattle can appreciate how crayfish claws and mussel shells could become a powerful source of exchange. Only someone who has taken smoked lobster claws, wrapped them with bark, fastened them around waist and ankles, and danced all night can understand this.

STEVEN FELD

A sick boy is being treated by five healers, all of whom sing. Each holds eagle feathers and pieces of straw in his left hand, and plays a rattle with his right. [New Mexico, ca. 1889]

In a Guinea legend, a goddess gave a rattle to Arawonity as he was walking by the riverside brooding over the troubles and miseries of humanity. A female form, the crehu, arose from the stream bearing in her hand a small branch which she presented to him. Desiring him to plant it and afterwards gather the fruit, he did so, and the fruit of the tree was the calabash. The second time she did arise from the stream — this time with some white stones in her hand, and she told him to enclose them in a gourd. He did so, and this made a maraca. It is under this ancient name that the gourd rattle survives in the modern Latin-American orchestra.

JOHN FREDERICK ROWBATHAM
(1893)

Shaman José Panco holds a rattle and a deertail. Papago Indians go to their healers when disease causes them to seek remedy. The shaman discovers what natural force the patient has harmed, then corrects the mishap by singing a song to realign the patient's relationship to that force. [Arizona, ca. 1920]

My grandfather gave me the rawhide thong to tie
     and the songs to use, and the long sinew
     cord to tie the toes.

My grandfather, I am tied by medicine power.

My grandfather gave me a whistle which
     has medicine power.

My grandfather gave me a tipi; the
     medicine wind makes it rock
     back and forth on the earth.

My grandfather gave me a rattle which
     has medicine power.

My grandfather gave me the night.

My grandfather gave me everything on this earth.

**BOB-TAILED WOLF,
CHEYENNE SHAMAN (1935)**

**Péhriska-Rúhpa,
a leader in the
warriors-only Dog
Society of the
Hidatsa people,
Upper Missouri
River, North Dakota,
donned ceremonial
regalia for this
portrait. His dew-
claw rattle is made
from deer hooves.**
[*Péhriska-Rúhpa*, by
Carl Bodmer, United
States, 1834]

Tawurawãnã **ritual is enacted with a sacred rattle and stamping tube, accompanying ritual songs among the Kamayurá Indians of the High Xingu.** [Brazil, probably mid-twentieth century]

*W*here shamanism comes to an end or women no longer shake the rattle in their original feminine rites, they leave it to infants as an irresistibly fascinating toy — its way from places of worship to cribs in the nursery is but one step.

CURT SACHS

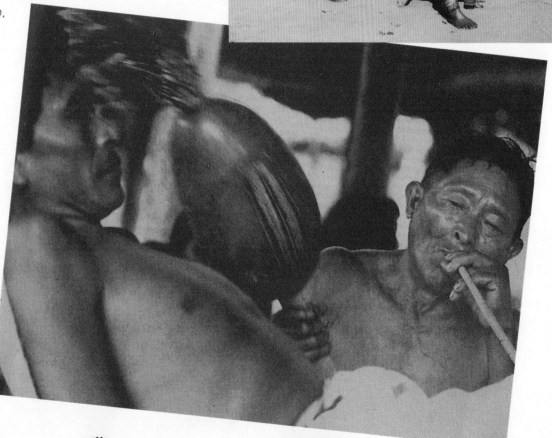

The Warao shaman intoxicates himself with a massive dose of nicotine from potent tobacco of the Orinoco River delta region. He chants and shakes the rattle over his patient. As the stones, the shaman's spiritual family, dance inside the rattle, sparks fly out through the slits, evidence of supernatural forces coming to treat the patient. [Venezuela, ca. 1960]

Rhythms of Life and Death

Sacrifice

Captain Cook looks on (at right) as a human sacrifice is prepared for a fiery end. [Drawing by John Webber, 1777]

Sacrifice is a key component in ritual. Something must always be given up, offered up, if commerce between this world and the spirit one is to continue amicably. In its extreme form, the sacrifice consists of one or more human beings, particularly the victims of intertribal warfare.

As André Schaeffner has written, "The construction and even the upkeep of drums can demand the use of blood, particularly human blood, poured either on the body or on the skin of the drum. From this originates special sacrificial rites. Among the Banyankole, in Uganda, at the time of the coronation of a new king, the royal drums are covered with new skin; the blood of a young boy is mixed with that of a cow and papyrus ashes, and the mixture is made into balls with which the drum is rubbed. In Dutch New Guinea the skin of the drum is glued with a mixture of lime and blood coming in part from the virile member." In other cultures, musicians must feed the spirits of their instruments with prayers, liquor, even food.

According to a contemporary account of one of his journeys across the Pacific in the eighteenth century, Captain Cook was able to take advantage of his own importance as a friend of the chief and witness one of the great Tahitian ceremonies, that of a human sacrifice. "When they arrived on the small point of land, the seamen were confined to the boat." Before them were many men, some boys, no women; priests, attendants, the great sacrificial drums and those who beat them; the bruised corpse trussed to a pole in a small canoe at the sea's edge, some miserable man caught unaware and felled with a stone. The ceremony began at once, a long and complicated affair of prayers and invocations, the production of symbolical articles, the symbolical eating of one of the victim's eyes by Tu, the offering to Oro of red feathers, some of the victim's hairs, the dog's entrails, the sounding of the drums."

THE SOUL OF THE GREAT BELL

CHINA

The water clock marks the hour in the Tower of the Great Bell. Now the mallet is lifted to smite the lips of the metal monster. ❧ KO-NGAI! ❧ All the little dragons on the high tilted eves of the green roofs shiver to the tips of their gilded tails. All the porcelain gargoyles tremble on their carved perches. All the hundred little bells in the pagodas quiver with desire to speak. ❧ KO-NGAI! ❧ For five hundred years the Great Bell has sounded thus, that thunderous golden KO-NGAI followed by a silvery, whispery, "hiai." For five hundred years these sounds have made the lacquered goblins on the palace cornices wriggle their fire colored tongues. ❧ KO-NGAI! ❧ Hiai. ❧ There is not a child in all the many-colored ways of this old Chinese city who does not know the story of the Great Bell, who cannot tell a passing traveler why the Great Bell says only Ko-ngai and Hiai. ❧ It happened five hundred years ago, when Yong-Lo, the Son of Heaven, commanded the worthy official, Kouan-Yu, to build a bell of such size and power that its voice might be heard for one hundred li. And he further commanded that the voice of this bell should be strengthened with brass, deepened with gold, and sweetened with silver, and that it should be suspended in the center of the imperial capital, so that its sound might travel along all the many colored ways of the city of Pe-King. ❧ The worthy Kouan-Yu, eager to do his Lord's bidding, assembled all the master moulders and bellsmiths in the empire. He hired the most cunning foundrymen. And they labored like giants, neglecting all the comforts of life, toiling day and night to produce the magnificent Great Bell that the son of Heaven desired. ❧ But when the earthen moulds were removed from the bell, it was discovered that the metals had rebelled against one another: the gold had scorned the brass, the silver had refused to mingle with the molten iron. ❧ They would have to try again. ❧ The Son of Heaven heard of their failure and was angry, but said nothing. ❧ A second time the bell was cast. The result was even worse than before. Not only were the metals unblended, but the sides were cracked and fissured. When the Son of Heaven heard of this second failure, he sent a messenger to Kouan-Yu with a letter written upon lemon-colored silk and sealed with the seal of a dragon. ❧ After the opening pleasantries, the letter got brutally to the point: "Twice thou hast betrayed the trust we have deigned graciously to place in thee; if thou fail a third time in fulfilling our command, thy head shall be severed from thy neck. Tremble and obey!" ❧ Now Kouan-Yu had a daughter of dazzling loveliness whose name, Ko-Ngai, was ever on the lips of the poets of Pe-King. But Ko-Ngai loved her father, loved him with such a deep, abiding affection that she had refused a hundred worthy suitors rather than make his home lonely with her absence. Upon learning of the emperor's threat, Ko-Ngai fainted dead away. ❧ When she regained her senses, she found herself unable to eat or sleep, so worried was she about her father's peril. Secretly she sold some of her jewels and consulted a famed astrologer, hoping that his magic and wisdom might show her a way to save her father. The famed astrologer examined the heavens. He marked the position of the Silver Stream, which we call the Milky Way. He scrutinized the signs of the Zodiac and consulted the table of the Five Hin, or Principles of the Universe. He even dipped into the writings of the alchemists. Finally he said to Ko-Ngai: "Gold and brass will never meet in wedlock, silver and iron will never embrace, until the flesh of a maiden be melted in the crucible, until the blood of a virgin be mixed with the metals in their fusion." ❧ Ko-Ngai returned home with a heavy, sorrowful heart. She told no one what she had done, nor what she had heard. ❧ At last came the horrible day when the third and last effort to cast the great bell was to occur. Ko-Ngai, together with her waiting women, accompanied her father to the foundry, and they took their places upon a platform overlooking the toiling moulders. No one spoke, not even the workmen. Only the crackling of the fires broke the stillness. ❧ At last the moment came for Kouan-Yu to give the signal to cast the bell. The metals were at their hottest, blood red and gold and silver. As he raised his hand to give the signal, a cry broke out and the voice of Ko-Ngai, as sweet as a bird's song above the thundering fires, cried out, "For thy sake, O my father." And even as she cried, to everyone's horror, she leaped into the molten metal and was consumed by the roar of the furnace. ❧ Kouan-Yu, wild with grief, would have leapt after her had he not been restrained by strong men who held him until he fainted and had to be carried home like one who was dead. Equally insensible with grief was Ko-Ngai's serving maid, who had tried to grab her as she jumped but had succeeded only in clutching one of Ko-Ngai's pretty shoes, a tiny, dainty shoe, embroidered with pearls and flowers. ❧ In spite of this tragedy, the command of the Son of Heaven had to be obeyed, and so the work went forward. The bell was cast. And lo! When the metal was cooled and the moulds removed, it was discovered that the bell was perfect and beautiful and its tone, when they sounded it, was deeper and mellower and mightier than any other bell in the Kingdom, audible even beyond the mandated distance of one hundred li, like a peal of summer thunder. And yet the sound also seemed to be like someone calling a name, the name of Ko-Ngai, and between each mighty stroke a low moaning could be heard, ending with a sobbing sound as though a weeping woman were murmuring "hiai." ❧ Even today, when the people hear the Great Bell, they remain silent until they hear that final sobbing "hiai" and then all the Chinese mothers in all the many-colored ways of Pe-King whisper to their little ones, "Listen! That is Ko-Ngai crying for her shoe! That is Ko-Ngai crying for her shoe!"

Possession

Possession trance is the psychic comple-ment of shamanic trance. Instead of the shaman riding the drumbeat up out of his body to the spirit world, in the possession trance the spirits ride the drumbeat down into the body of the trance dancer. While a shaman is able to give a lucid account of his or her adventures at the edge, the possessed person remembers nothing; is, in fact, an empty vessel that the god temporarily fills.

Variations of possession trance can be found in cultures around the globe, but they have achieved perhaps their richest articulation in West Africa. There an ancestor spirit is known as an *Orisha* — literally "he whom Ori [the head] has picked out for distinction." It is said that anyone who does something so great that it can never be forgotten can become an *Orisha*. Some, like Ogun and Shango, have become so famous and powerful that their status approaches the godlike.

It is the drum that calls the *Orisha*. They are said to respond to different rhythms: their signature beat guides them down into the body of the dancer to assume control.

Some scholars connect the West African possession cultures with the ancient Neolithic mother goddess culture that nine thousand years ago stretched from eastern Europe into what is now the Sahara desert. When the slave trade began in the seventeenth century, this technique of possession trance was carried to the New World. In those places where the Africans were allowed to keep their drums, it mutated into candomblé, santería, and vôdun. In America, where the drums were prohibited for many gen-erations, this legacy of possession-trance dance rhythm was shorn of its spiritual dimension, becoming instead jazz, blues, rhythm and blues, and rock and roll.

Accompanied by the drums of the vôdun ritual, the man at left is pos-sessed by the *loa* (spirit) of Dambala, a snake spirit be-lieved to be the positive force that encircles the uni-verse. [Haiti, 1946] ▶

The woman dancer is in a possession trance, part of a larger community ritual. [Ivory Coast, ca. 1981]

Nothing could be more striking…than the contrast one can observe among the Wolof of Senegal between the behavior of the marabouts who seek out ecstasy in the silence, solitude, and darkness of their grottos and that of the practitioners of the ndöp, *who enter into trance in the midst of a dense crowd, stimulated by drink, agitated by wild dancing and the din of drums.*

GILBERT ROUGET

DIVINE HORSEMEN

In the terminology of Voudoun, it is said that the loa "mounts" a person, or that a person is "mounted" by the loa. The metaphor is drawn from a horse and his rider and the actions and events which result are the expression of the will of the rider. Since the conscious self of the possessed person is, meanwhile, absent, he cannot and does not remember the events; he is not responsible, either for good or for bad; and he cannot, as a person, himself benefit from that possession. The function and purpose of such divine manifestation is the reassurance and instruction of the community.

The drummer…becomes, to some degree, the arbiter of the loa's arrival.… When the drummer is particularly gifted and acute, he can permit the tension to build to just the level where the "break" serves not to release tension but to climax it in a galvanizing shock — the first enormous blow of the "break" — which abruptly empties the head and leaves one without any center around which to stabilize. This is a state of helpless vulnerability. Instead of being able to move in the long, balanced strides of relaxation, the defenseless person is buffeted by each great stroke, as the drummer sets out to "beat the loa into his head." The person cringes with each large beat, as if the drum mallet descended

upon his very skull; he ricochets about the peristyle, clutching blindly at the arms which are extended to support him, pirouettes wildly on one leg, recaptures balance for a brief moment, only to be hurtled forward again by another great blow on the drum. The drummer, apparently impervious to the embattled anguish of the person, persists relentlessly; until, suddenly, the violence ceases, the head of the person lifts, and one recognizes the strangely abstracted eyes of a being who seems to see beyond whatever he looks at, as if into or from another world. The loa which the song had been invoking, has arrived.

MAYA DEREN

Rhythms of Life and Death

139

Carnaval!

Pandeiro. [Rio de Janeiro, Brazil, 1981]

A *ritmista* (musician-dancer) twirls a *pandeiro*. [Rio de Janeiro, Brazil, 1981]

Carnaval is a party, a parade, and a festival all rolled into one. The week before Lent, the inhibitions and daily cares of life are forgotten and people hit the streets for an endless round of drumming, dancing, and drinking. The name *carnaval* comes from a Latin expression meaning "to take away meat" and is the only aspect of the festival that's derived from the Christian tradition of Lent; everything else comes from ancient African and American Indian fertility and planting rituals onto which the Christians grafted their pre-Easter rites.

Surdo. [Rio de Janeiro, Brazil, 1985]

Festive celebrants play a *pandeiro.* [Rio de Janeiro, Brazil, 1981]

Some form of *carnaval* **is celebrated wherever the Catholic festival of Lent is observed.** [Port of Spain, Trinidad, 1888]

Planet Drum

The *cuica*, **friction drum, is played in tandem.** [Rio de Janeiro, Brazil, 1981]

A *surdo* – a large, double-headed metal drum – is played at *carnaval.*
[Rio de Janeiro, Brazil, 1981]

CHAPTER FOUR

SCULPTURES OF SOUND

145

Taiko **drums, played
by members of
Kodo.** [Sado Island,
Japan, mid-1980s]

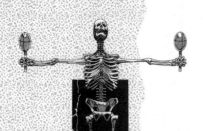

THE SKINS AND LACINGS, THE WOODEN BODIES —
these were not made to endure. Dampness swells and cracks
them. The paint fades. Fire destroys them in seconds. Consequently, we have few percussion instruments that are more than
two hundred years old. ❧ Yet enough remain to illustrate our
ancient desire to construct a varied soundscape around the
simple acts of striking, scraping, shaking. Some of these instruments are gigantic, like the huge slit-gongs, the volcanic rock
harmonica, and the bass drum that is bigger than the tallest
man. Some were made to adorn the houses and palaces of the
rich and powerful. Some tell a symbolic story. Some set a beat
for tribes or villages to dance to, some provided music for theater, a feast, a celebration. Some sounded only in the most august
political or religious rituals. ❧ Nearly all of them, from the
plainest rattle to the most ornate ritual drum, were made to be
played by hand. Except for bells, these percussion instruments
remained human-scale, imaginative extensions of the human
body that mirror the universe of rhythm surrounding us. ❧ ❧

Membranophones

Membranophone – literally "skin sound"– is a Latin word and a Greek word combined into one. It describes the instrument made by stretching a skin of animal, vegetable, or man-made material so that when it vibrates it produces sound. Tom-tom, timpani, tambourine – almost all drums fall into this class.

One of the largest double-headed bass drums in the world was made for Walt Disney Productions by Remo, Inc. This enormous drum, 10½ feet tall and 40 inches wide, dwarfs manufacturer Remo Belli, shown playing the traps. [California, 1961]

The *pahu*, a dance drum, accompanies religious dances at outdoor temples. The arches in the base probably represent mythological supports for the sky. [Hawaii, probably twentieth century]

DHARMA DRUM

The big drum, called ngo, *is round to symbolize the universe, and empty within to symbolize the dharma (teaching). When we sound the drum it symbolizes spreading dharma throughout the universe. A dragon and a calf are painted on the frame of the drum. The dragon relates to the biggest sounds, thundering loudly all over the universe.*

The music is to attract the attention of the deities, and to give them pleasure. Deities exist on a larger scale than humans, and we try to entertain them with appropriate music.

We always say it's like having an important guest in one's house, such as a king or nobleman. You greet them politely, give them a cool drink, offer some fruit, sit down for some food, and then provide music to entertain them. Only later do you ask for favors or assistance. Entertainment first.

The purpose of the rituals is to host the deities properly, to entice them into your house, entertain them, then finally to give them your prayerful message, and send them away on their mission—such as protecting all living beings, putting a stop to war, hunger, or similar beneficial action.

TARTHANG TULKU

The drum-harmonica was a novelty item advertised in a mail-order catalog early in this century. The sound of the harmonica was amplified by the shell and membrane of the drum. [United States, ca. 1906]

Drum Harmonica Triumphator

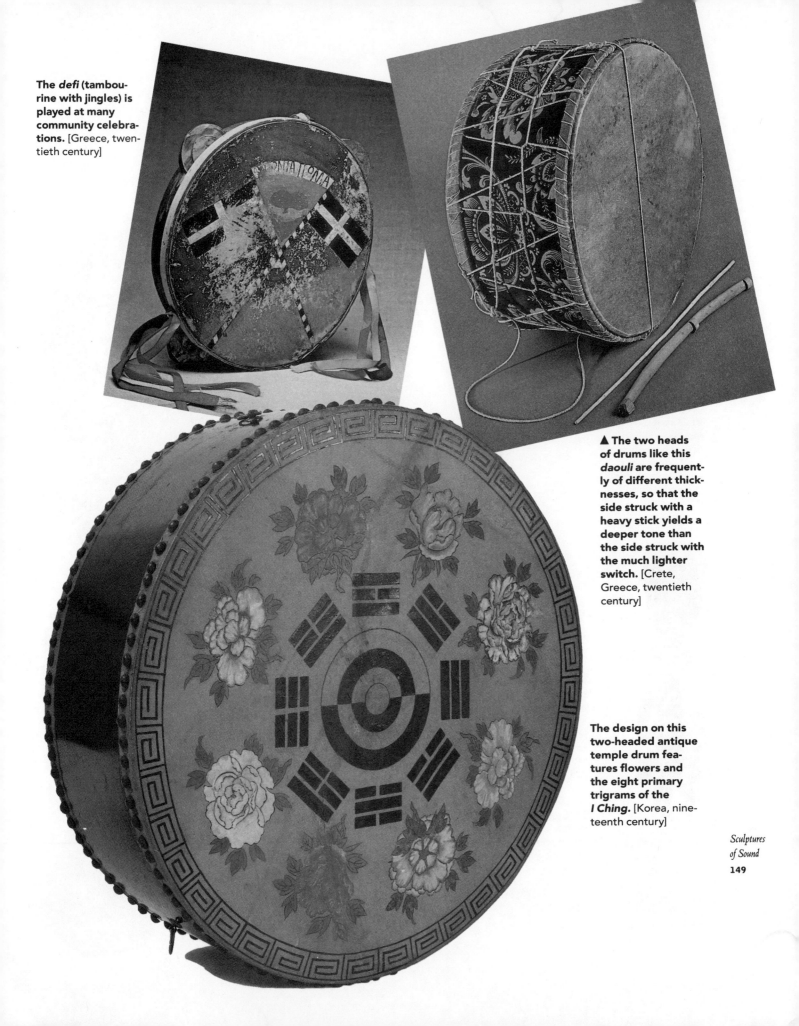

The *defi* (tambourine with jingles) is played at many community celebrations. [Greece, twentieth century]

▲ The two heads of drums like this *daouli* are frequently of different thicknesses, so that the side struck with a heavy stick yields a deeper tone than the side struck with the much lighter switch. [Crete, Greece, twentieth century]

The design on this two-headed antique temple drum features flowers and the eight primary trigrams of the *I Ching*. [Korea, nineteenth century]

Leonardo da Vinci sketched this mechanical kettle-drum that would beat continuously when pulled along in a procession. [Milan, Italy, ca. 1490]

Planet Drum

150

This drum sits on the head of a man who sits on a leopard. A child sits on the lap of the man and both play on a small drum. [Vili people, Loandjili, Zaire, nineteenth century]

▶ This Persian *dombak*, covered with geometric and symbolic inlay, was probably a royal or court instrument. The *dombak* is the most important percussion instrument in Persian traditional music. The head is usually fish or animal skin. The body is carved from a single log. [Iran, probably eighteenth century]

As a symbol of peace and friendship, Japan sent this ornate *ō-daiko* drum and stand to the Vienna Exposition of 1873. It was not intended to be used as a performance instrument.

◄ The eagle/human figure decorating this *huehuetl* probably represents Quetzalcoatl, an Aztec deity who, with an eagle's aid, founded Mexico City. [Malinalco, Mexico, fifteenth century]

► Drums of the coastal Senufo are known for their elaborate carving. The animals and humans on this *pliéwo* are familiar characters in Senufo cosmology and are seen in many of their decorative arts. [Mali or Ivory Coast, twentieth century]

A drummer gives the rhythm to a tree. [Geré people, Ivory Coast, 1964]

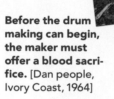

Before the drum making can begin, the maker must offer a blood sacrifice. [Dan people, Ivory Coast, 1964]

Making the Drum

Because they can animate the voices of otherwise mute materials like wood, bamboo, stone, gourd, bone, and clay, musical instruments are often treated as power objects, and the people who make them are seen as guardians of great and mysterious secrets. Consequently, the process of making an instrument is one of ritual precision, characterized by offerings to the spirit of the tree or animal whose parts are being transformed.

The technology employed in making musical instruments is frequently the most sophisticated known to the culture — such as the techniques used for casting the large bronze bells in ancient China or the meticulous attention that many cultures pay to the tanning of the animal hides that will be used as drumheads. While found materials such as naturally hollow logs may be used for drum bodies, more often the wood is selected for size, grain, toughness, resistance to cracking or warping, and other acoustic and structural properties. It is then aged appropriately, hollowed, and carved.

Great care is given to each stage of the making of the drum.
[Dan people, Ivory Coast, 1964]

Bullroarers

The bullroarer is most often made from a flat piece of wood, bone, or metal, with an attached rope. The player swings the bullroarer lasso-like over the head, which causes the instrument not just to revolve around the musician, but also to spin quickly on its own axis, producing an incomparable humming or buzzing sound.

A bullroarer in action over a corpse at a funeral. [Senufo people, Ivory Coast, 1965]

Bullroarer

The bullroarer, which is a child's toy in our culture, still figures as an important sacred object in Oceania, Africa, and America.... Saglio cites a text that talks of "a small piece of wood ... which is shaken in the air to make it make noise"; this was certainly a bullroarer, and probably the rhomboi used in the mysteries of Bacchus and Cybele. But these ancient texts don't distinguish it well from its other form, the diable, a little disk of wood, stone, or metal with two holes through which a string is passed that twists and untwists as one pulls on the ends. This twisting movement causes the diable to rotate and make its growling sound. Women of antiquity used this instrument as a love charm. In all of these cases it is an instrument that rotates and makes a humming sound.

We have no choice but to be struck that such different cultures attribute power to the sound of a thin disk or fish-shaped object being rotated. In places where it hasn't become a simple toy, or, as in Malaysia, something to scare away wild beasts and elephants, the bullroarer is a particularly taboo object—except in extremely rare cases—strictly hidden from women and noninitiates, that is believed to emit the voice of a spirit.

In Australia and New Guinea it is the voice of a monster that will carry off young people, eat them and spit them back out into life metamorphosed into men, that is to say, circumcised and initiated. Only initiates know that the noise in question comes from a simple bullroarer. Certain tribes of northern New Guinea build a hut thirty meters long in the shape of a monster: "The enormous creature produces a ferocious growling, which is nothing other than the sound of bullroarers being swung by men hidden in the belly of the beast." Identified one place with the sound of the monster, other places with the cry of the largest masque, the sound of the bullroarer is equally associated with the voice of the ancestors. It is the grandfather, the spirit of the dead, and in Cameroon it is even kept with the skulls of the ancestors.

About the invention of the bullroarer, the Warramunga of Australia tell that "two wild dogs, having heard the sound made by Murtu-murtu with his mouth, jumped on him and tore him to pieces, which they threw in all directions. These pieces, when they split the air, made a sound like that of the bullroarer."

This myth of creation reminds us of the kinship between the boomerang and the bullroarer, either that the bullroarer was originally in the shape of a boomerang, or else that bullroarers were spun without attached strings.

ANDRÉ
SCHAEFFNER

BULLROARER NAMES

Say the names aloud. Listen to the sound.

NAME	REGION	NAME	REGION
abume	Tiv people, Nigeria	kode	Maninka people, Guinea
arib	Irian Jaya, Papua New Guinea	kundrukundru	Adoi, Amanga, Andebogo, and
arumvurumvu	Mamvu people, Zaire		Andowi peoples, Zaire
atuamba	Kuma people, Zaire	kunzukunzu	Aimeri people, Zaire
balum	Bukaua and Yabem peoples, Papua	kwese	Dakakari people, Nigeria
	New Guinea	liahan	Buka, Solomon Islands
baranga	Vere people, Nigeria	luvuvu	Kiwai people, Papua New Guinea
bimbi	Sango people, Zaire	manggasieng	Minangkabau, West Sumatra
bora	Borli people, Papua New Guinea	mbirimbiri	Mayogo people, Zaire
botagas	Lithuania, Soviet Union	ngetundo	Nandi people, Kenya
brüklys	Lithuania, Soviet Union	ngosa	Kai people, Papua New Guinea
bui	Mawai people, Papua New Guinea	oeoe	Hawaii
buro	Florida Island, Solomon Islands	oro	Yoruba people, Nigeria and Benin
burubush	Khoikhoi people, South Africa	oupa	Nyali people, Zaire
burunga	Maria people, Madhya Pradesh, India	ower-ower	Central Java, Indonesia
butkidis	Lithuania, Soviet Union	peer boor egah	Australia
cri de la belle-mère	France	puurorohuu	Maori people, New Zealand
dengeng-dengeng	Batak Toba district, North Sumatra	riwi-riwi loco	Nias, Indonesia
diable des bois	France	rofla	Limousin, France
egburuburu	Mamvu people, Zaire	seburuburu	Tswana people, Botswana
epop	Kosrae, Caroline Islands	sevevu	Southern Sotho people, Lesotho
ereg-ereg	Central Java, Indonesia	sosom	Marindanim and Tugeri peoples,
gilingwa	Zande people, Zaire		Papua New Guinea
goingoing	San people, southwestern Africa	tangalop	Tanga Island, Papua New Guinea
guev	North Bougainville, Solomon Islands	tarabilla	Argentina
gueyoumo	Kono people, Guinea	tepoanim gongui	Papua New Guinea
hevehe	Orokolo people, Papua New Guinea	tiparu	Toaripi people, Papua New Guinea
imillutaq	Inuit people, Canada	tomlulur	Tanga Island, Papua New Guinea
inano	Mbole people, Zaire	tshihwilili	Venda people, South Africa
jata	Ende region, Flores, Indonesia	tsinidi'ni'	Navajo people, United States
juco	Nicaragua	tuambi	Kuma people, Zaire
kabara	Achipawa people, Nigeria	ual ual	Mohave Apache people, United States
kani	Tami Island, Papua New Guinea	umbubu	Orokaiva people, Papua New Guinea
kekinciran	West Java, Indonesia	wer-wer	Central Java, Indonesia
kgabudubudu	Pedi people, Lesotho	wuwu	Koko people, Papua New Guinea
khabulubulu	Southern Sotho people, Lesotho	zugattyu	Hungary

Idiophones

Idiophone is the general term for musical instruments that "produce their sound from the substance of the instrument itself, being solid or elastic enough not to require stretched membranes or strings," says *Grove's Dictionary of Musical Instruments.* Slit-drums, castanets, bells, gongs, scrapers and rattles, the glass harmonica and other oddities, all are members of this huge group of musical instruments.

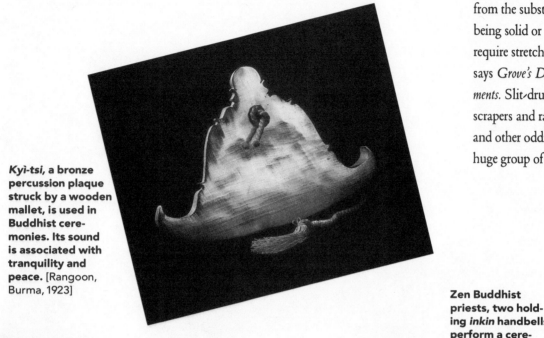

Kyì-tsi, a bronze percussion plaque struck by a wooden mallet, is used in Buddhist ceremonies. Its sound is associated with tranquility and peace. [Rangoon, Burma, 1923]

Zen Buddhist priests, two holding *inkin* handbells, perform a ceremony. A *mokugyo* temple block is at right, a *kin* bell at left. [Japan, 1960s]

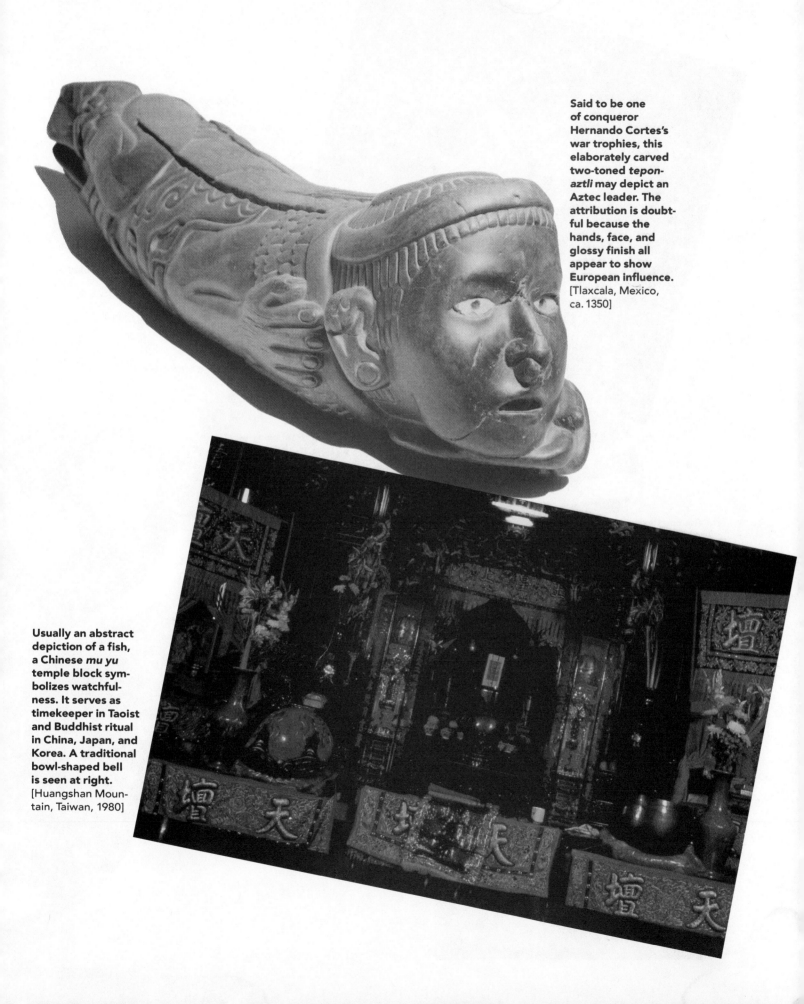

Said to be one of conqueror Hernando Cortes's war trophies, this elaborately carved two-toned *teponaztli* may depict an Aztec leader. The attribution is doubtful because the hands, face, and glossy finish all appear to show European influence. [Tlaxcala, Mexico, ca. 1350]

Usually an abstract depiction of a fish, a Chinese *mu yu* temple block symbolizes watchfulness. It serves as timekeeper in Taoist and Buddhist ritual in China, Japan, and Korea. A traditional bowl-shaped bell is seen at right. [Huangshan Mountain, Taiwan, 1980]

This African rattle is made of millet stalks strung around a calabash. [Savannah region, West/central Africa, date unknown]

The drive to create, perform and reproduce music is common to all mankind. A drive so basic that when a man cannot find an instrument to suit him, he creates his own.

JOSEPH HOWARD

The smaller pair of these sets of hand cymbals is made of nickel-plated brass and the larger of bronze. [Greece, twentieth century]

This shaman's rattle is made in the shape of a raven. [Tlingit people, Alaska, date unknown]

Planet Drum

158

A slit-gong carved from an enormous tree was placed in a field outside the royal palace and beaten to announce war, to gather the people, or to accompany festivals. [Bamum people, Foumban, Cameroon, ca. 1903]

This peyote gourd (rattle) and parrot fan are used in Native American church ceremonies. [Made by Richard Dobson, California, 1987] ▼

Sculptures of Sound

A nineteenth-century British handbill proclaims: *Richardsons' Original Monstre Rock Band Invented and manufactured by Messrs Richardson and Sons* after 13 years' incessant labour and application from rocks dug out of the mighty Skiddaw in Cumberland (1827–40)

A blind woman, Angelica Kaufmann, plays the armonica, or glasschord, an instrument invented by Benjamin Franklin. Music was composed for it by Mozart, Beethoven, and others. [Engraving by anonymous artist, Germany, 1819]

The gourd water-drum consists of an inverted half-gourd floating in a larger half-gourd partly filled with water. The smaller half-gourd emits a clear and low-pitched tone when struck. [Malinke people, Papua New Guinea, second half of twentieth century]

From one material to the next, the construction of instruments eventually embraces all of nature. As Combarieu remarks, musical instruments put into the hands of the magician "parcels of all the kingdoms of nature: they are made of rosewood or bamboo, pods of certain fruits, metal, hardwood, sonorous stone, animal skins, shells, bone, horns, silk, twisted raffia, tendons, gut...; they constitute a summary of the cosmos."

ANDRÉ SCHAEFFNER

The shining water that moves in the streams and rivers is not just water, but the blood of our ancestors....The water's murmur is the voice of my father's father. The rivers are our brothers. They quench our thirst. They carry our canoes and feed our children. So you must give to the rivers the kindness you would give any brother.

CHIEF SEATTLE,
SUQUAMISH PEOPLE

Using their cupped hands to strike the water, these 'Are'Are women are having fun creating complex rhythmic patterns. [Malaita, Solomon Islands, mid-1960s]

When bells were not allowed to ring, this ratchet was sounded in church during the Holy Week remembrance of Christ's betrayal, crucifixion, and resurrection. [France, ca. fourteenth century]

Noise-making percussion instruments – like the ratchet, bones, castanets, whirring disc, and xylophone – have long been believed to dispel evil by frightening away malevolent spirits or attracting benevolent ones. [Europe, nineteenth century]

Sculptures of Sound

161

Bells, Voices of Metal

Crack two sticks together. Strike skin — either your own or that of a drum — with the palm of your hand. Shake a rattle. Beat a hollow log. The unity in the sound of all these percussive acts is transformed when the material becomes metal.

The bell is a mutation of the drum, one that has gone on to achieve a different kind of percussive grandeur. Whereas the sound of a drumbeat sprays out in a wide range of frequencies, the "bong" of a bell or gong vibrates in several narrow ranges, one high-pitched and clanging, the other low and droning. This last effect, that long low drone, is what makes the bell an indifferent instrument for articulating rhythm, but a wonderful one for producing loud and lengthy noise.

Sounding metals are found all over the world. Wherever metal technology took root, the culture produced some form of bell or gong, ranging in size from delicate pebble-sized bells to the monstrous Tsar-Kolokol of Russia, at 433,000 pounds humanity's greatest achievement in bronze casting.

The fascination with big bells was particularly strong in East Asia and the Christian West. Elevated in towering church steeples, high above the busy streets of medieval Europe, bells became the primary pulse of the city, the timekeeper, the community heartbeat. It is said that travelers would weep with happiness when they heard from a distance the familiar sound of their hometown bells.

In the Christian West, the sound of the church bell supplanted the sound of the drum as the channel of the spirit. The resonant roar of the bell was our metaphor for the voice of God.

Huge bells do not drive the body to dance, but they do seem to activate certain emotions. The low drone, for example, is said to impart a feeling of tranquillity, awe, and finality, while the high-pitched clang appeals to another order of emotions. Together, this harmonic mix is said to clear the mind, uplift the spirit, and invite a look to the heavens for guidance and communion.

Frogs, horse-back riders, and a bird ring this elaborately engraved bronze drumhead around the central star. Frogs, harbingers of spring, are considered symbols of fertility by many cultures. [China, ca. 200 B.C.]

Tumbaga, the small (less than two inches high) gilded bells of the Incas, are made of an alloy that is 30 percent gold and 70 percent copper. [Colombia, early sixteenth century]

This anthropomorphic cast bronze bell is from the kingdom of Benin. [Nigeria, probably eighteenth century]

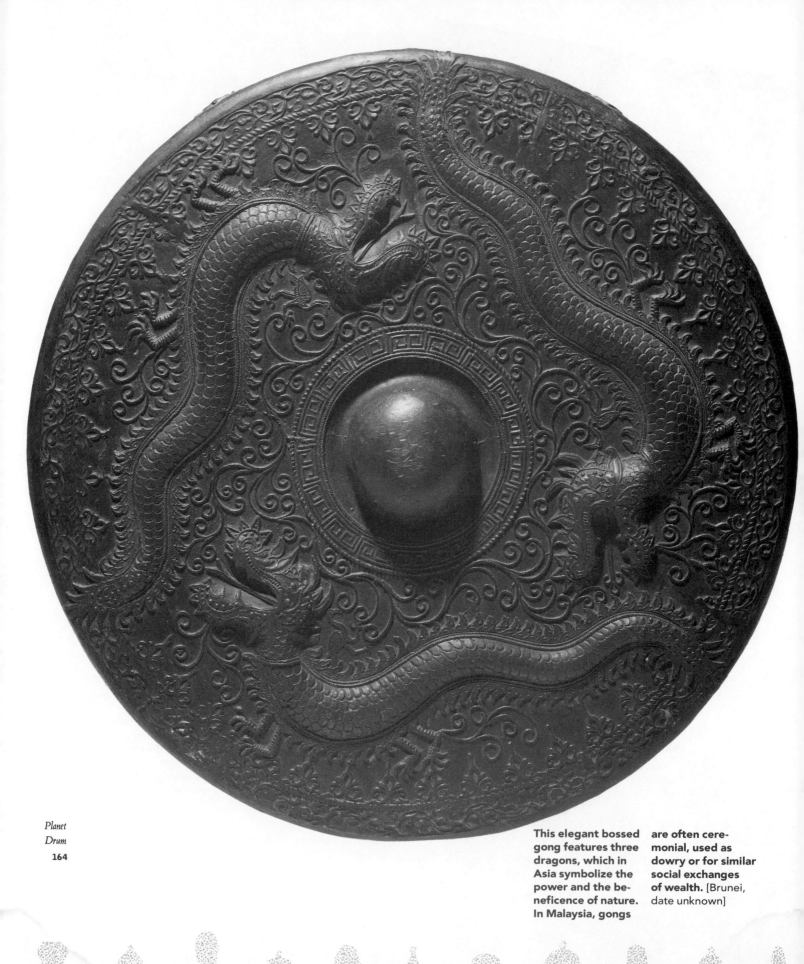

This elegant bossed gong features three dragons, which in Asia symbolize the power and the beneficence of nature. In Malaysia, gongs are often ceremonial, used as dowry or for similar social exchanges of wealth. [Brunei, date unknown]

The dramatic vista of bells in Hamburg, Germany, during World War II, vividly demonstrates the continuing relation between bells and cannons. Bells served as a repository of refined metals that could easily be melted down and recast as weapons. More than 100,000 bells were collected at the port of Hamburg.

During the fourteenth century, European metal foundries adapted bell-casting techniques to create "bombards," the first cannons. The early weapons in this illuminated manuscript look very much like upturned bells. [Europe, fifteenth century]

Geiji, small crotal bells, are tied to leather pads and used for rhythmic accent in ritual dance. [Ambalangoda, Sri Lanka, date unknown]

Two drum-shaped bronze sculptures from ancient China have been unearthed. These sculptures imitate wooden drums: the "drumheads" have been worked to resemble alligator skin, and sculpted nails show how the heads were attached to wooden bodies. Intricate geometric patterns and stylized animal masks spiral across both drums. [China, 1400–1100 B.C.]

TSAR-KOLOKOL

The critical moment in the casting of a bell has arrived as the stream of molten bronze is poured into the pit. [Yaroslavl, Russia, late nineteenth century]

The founding of the Tsar-Kolokol is the story of heroic invention and incredibly bad luck. In 1730, the empress of Russia, Anna, commissioned the casting of a bell that would dwarf all previous bells, not just in Russia but in all the world. The empress desired a bell that would surpass the greatest cathedral bells of Europe and the magnificent temple bells of Asia.

The commission was given to Ivan Motorin, Moscow's master bell maker. For four years he worked on this bell, aided by 180 workers. Over 350 tons of metal were melted down in preparation, but disaster struck on the night the bell was supposed to be cast. Three of the furnaces that were being used to heat the metal burst. The molten bronze flowed out, quickly setting the building ablaze, creating an inferno that destroyed everything. Brokenhearted, the master bell maker died the following year.

In 1735, the commission was then taken up by the bell maker's son, Mikhail. It took him a year to reduplicate his father's efforts. On the night he was ready to make the cast, four hundred Moscow fire fighters were standing by, just in case. This time the furnaces held. The molten metal was brought to the proper temperature and poured into the huge mold of the largest bell in the world — over nineteen feet high, weighing a staggering 433,000 pounds. Mikhail felt he had vindicated his father's faith in the possibility of founding a perfect bell of unparalleled size and weight.

But the casting was only the first step in the making of such a mammoth bell. For two years Mikhail labored over the preparations to raise it from the pit in which it had been cast. One night fire broke out in the city of Moscow. Within hours, much of the city was in flames, including the part of the Kremlin where the huge bell lay.

Soon the wooden shed that stood over the pit was ablaze. Burning timbers began tumbling down onto the bell. Firemen came rushing up with water. When the ice-cold water hit the red-hot surface of the bell, the metal expanded, popping off an enormous chip, as tall as one man, as wide as two, and weighing approximately 26,500 pounds.

The bell, which had acquired the name Tsar-Kolokol (meaning "emperor of bells"), was silenced forever.

Its creator, Mikhail Motorin, died in 1750. For another eighty years the bell lay in the subterranean darkness of its casting pit, nearly forgotten. In 1836 the French architect Auguste Ricard de Montferrand was commissioned to raise the giant bell and erect it as a monument to the power of the Russian rulers. As throngs of astonished citizens watched, Montferrand and his assembled work force of hundreds of soldiers and carpenters, successfully raised the Tsar-Kolokol, "like some enormous armored creature emerging out of the earth." With enormous effort, the bell was rolled on logs up to a granite pedestal and the "chip" was propped against its base.

By 1849 the interior of the Tsar-Kolokol had been consecrated as a chapel and Russians could enter into the bell's enormous cavity to worship. It stands today in Kremlin Square, colossal testimony to humankind's obsession with bells.

The damaged Tsar-Kolokol after it was raised by Montferrand in 1836. Since that day, it has remained a silent monument. [Moscow, nineteenth century]

Skulls

The use of bones, especially human bone, or other parts of bodies of humans or certain other animals: skin, horn, hair, bristles, feathers, sinew, gut — exhibits another source of the relation between instrument making and magic. It seems obvious that whistling through a human femur or tibia, or using them to beat a drum, must have some influence on the sound produced or on the person who produces it.

ANDRÉ SCHAEFFNER

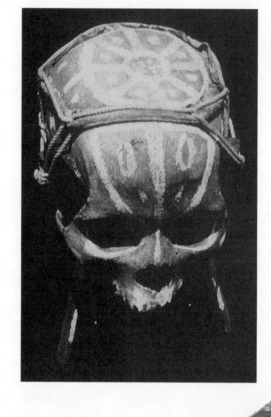

Used in funeral ceremonies by a high priest of the Abakua, a mystic brotherhood, the human skull drum is mounted on a base of three tibia bones. [Cuba, ca. 1850]

Two small *damarus*, one made of halved human skulls, the other of wood. [Tibet, late nineteenth or early twentieth century]

Buddhists don't get hung up on ancestral things. But an important reason that we use bones — both animal and human — in instruments such as the damaru, *the thigh-bone trumpets, and in implements such as skull bowls, is to serve as continual reminders of impermanence and the immediacy of death. You know that death is close by, and that death is an advisor. And you realize that your own bones will eventually be like this. Therefore, one learns to seek the essential in life, realizing the immanent presence of death.*

TARTHANG TULKU

PLANET DRUM

173

Sistra. [Lalibela, Ethiopia, mid-1980s]

THE MOST TIMID OF US FIND MAKING A LOUD noise on a drum intensely pleasurable. Wow! That was me – roaring like a lion! Drums are great instruments for building self-esteem. You can be loud and aggressive, using your whole body, and it's okay because you're not fighting or harming anything, you're just drumming. And if you keep it up for twenty or thirty minutes you'll probably feel very calm, very centered – a kind of drummer's high. But drums are more than just the means to make a loud noise. They are also tools for exploring rhythm, one of the deepest mysteries in the universe. Science has taught us that we live in a rhythmscape in which everything is pulsing in time with everything else. Every atom, every planet, every star is vibrating in a complex dance. We live on planet drum. And human beings, as multidimensional rhythm machines, are also embedded in this universe of rhythm. As a species we love to play with rhythm because it seems to connect us to something fundamental in the nature of reality. We deal with it every second of our lives, right to the very end, because when the rhythms stop, we die. These images are a testament to planet drum – to the magnitude of our pleasure at being able to control noise rhythmically. They reveal the joy, the agony, the power, and the mastery that is fundamental to the experience of percussion. Intent, totally focused faces contorted in concentration and effort – thus has the brotherhood and sisterhood of the drum maintained its beat throughout the ages.

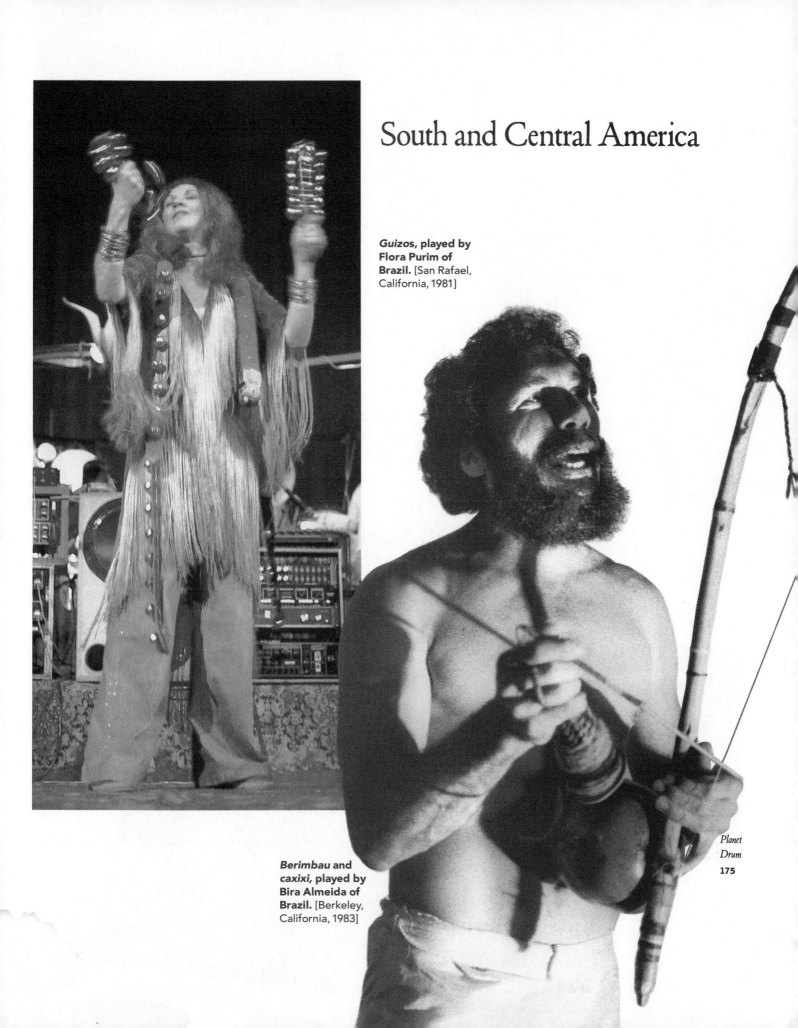

South and Central America

Guizos, **played by Flora Purim of Brazil.** [San Rafael, California, 1981]

Berimbau **and** *caxixi*, **played by Bira Almeida of Brazil.** [Berkeley, California, 1983]

Planet Drum

Pans (steel drums).
[Trinidad, late 1980s]

Tinya. [Huancavelica,
Peru, 1978]

Timbales, played
by Tito Puente.
[San Rafael, Califor-
nia, 1984]

Congas, played by Francisco Aguabella. [San Francisco, 1988]

Europe and North America

This French drummer was also the executioner of Louis the Sixteenth.
[France, nineteenth century]

Quasimodo (Charles Laughton) leaps to embrace his beloved bell in the classic film *The Hunchback of Notre Dame*, based on Victor Hugo's 1831 novel. The bell-ringing scene was shot just after England and France had declared war on Germany. The tension of the coming war filled the sound stage. At the end of the scene Laughton kept on ringing the bells until he was exhausted. He later said, "I couldn't think of Esmeralda in the scene at all. I could only think of the poor people out there, going to fight that bloody war! To arouse the world, to stop that terrible butchery! Awake! Awake! That's what I felt when I was ringing the bells!"
[United States, 1939]

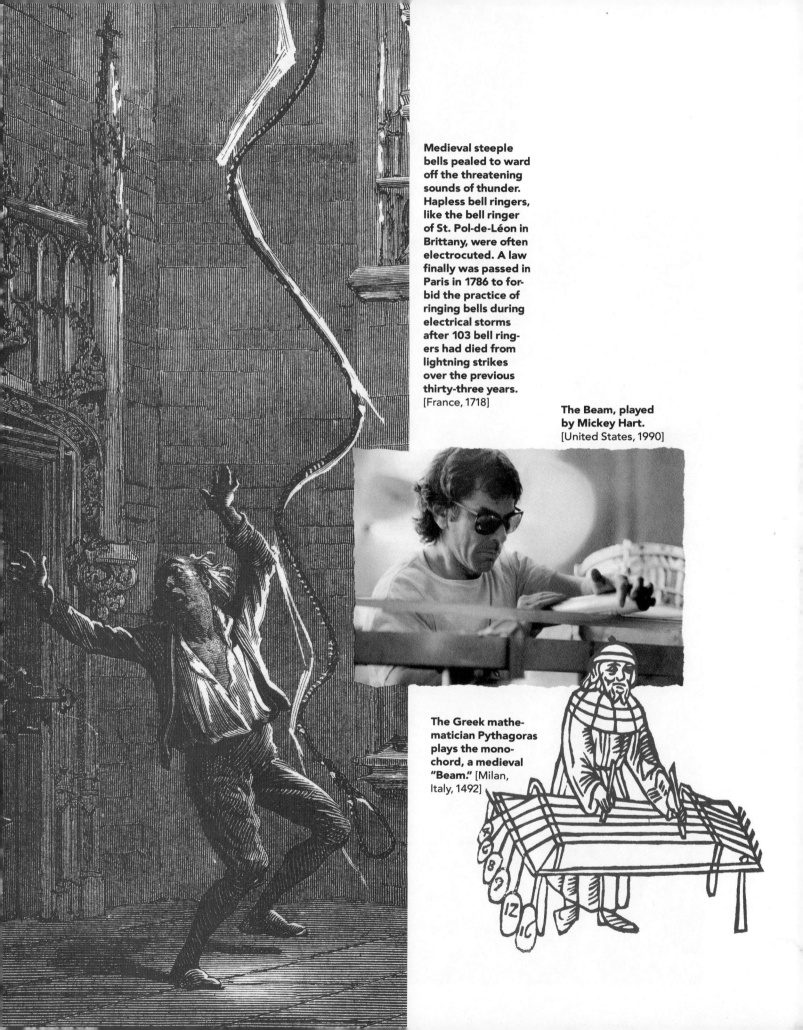

Medieval steeple bells pealed to ward off the threatening sounds of thunder. Hapless bell ringers, like the bell ringer of St. Pol-de-Léon in Brittany, were often electrocuted. A law finally was passed in Paris in 1786 to forbid the practice of ringing bells during electrical storms after 103 bell ringers had died from lightning strikes over the previous thirty-three years. [France, 1718]

The Beam, played by Mickey Hart. [United States, 1990]

The Greek mathematician Pythagoras plays the monochord, a medieval "Beam." [Milan, Italy, 1492]

Side drums, played by the City of Los Angeles Pipe Band. [Los Angeles, 1989]

Washboard, played by John "Mambo" Treanor. [San Francisco, 1990]

Tap dancer Skip
Cunningham taps
out a rhythm in the
1984 movie, *The
Cotton Club.*

Snare drums,
played by the UCLA
Drum Line. [Los
Angeles, 1989]

Tambourine, played
by Layne Redmond.
[New York, 1990]

▲ Barrel drum at Taos Pueblo. [New Mexico, 1907]

Barrel drum, played by a Dieguéño Indian. [California, 1909] ▼

Barrel drum at Laguna Pueblo. [New Mexico, ca. 1910]

***Sonazo* sistrum and cocoon ankle rattles, played by a Yaqui Indian.** [Mexico, 1940]

Planet Drum

183

Nearly a century ago, in the parishes around New Orleans, people began dancing to the new beat of jazz and the blues. Military drumming was too rigid to power these new rhythms. In their search for an answer to this problem, drummers began ransacking the percussive inventory. They took elements from all over the planet — snares and bass drums from Europe, the tom-tom from China, cymbals from Turkey — and along with such homely additions as cowbells, anvils, and woodblocks invented a new kind of drumming, and almost incidentally, a new instrument.

This hybrid was known as a "contraption," later shortened to "traps." Within twenty years virtuosos of the "traps" emerged, people like New Orleans jazz great Warren "Baby" Dodds, who worked with a bass drum, a snare, four cowbells, a cymbal, a tom-tom, and a woodblock. By the time the jazz age caught hold in the twenties, drum makers like the Ludwigs were already marketing formalized versions of the trap sets that drummers like Dodds had put together.

"Baby" Dodds (1898–1959). [United States, 1940]

Gene Krupa (1909–1973). [United States, 1956]

Chick Webb (1909–1939). [United States, ca. 1937]

Buddy Rich (1917–1987). [United States, 1950s]

Max Roach (b. 1924). [United States, ca. 1960]

Chico Hamilton (b. 1921). [United States, 1950s]

Louie Bellson (b. 1924). [Los Angeles, 1989]

Ginger Baker (b. 1940). [England, 1980s]

Billy Cobham (b. 1944). [Cagliari, Sardinia, Italy, 1978]

Keith Moon (1947–1978). [London, ca. 1975]

Ringo Starr (b. 1940). [England, ca. 1966]

Planet Drum
187

The Near East

Tars. [Doha, Qatar, 1988]

Tabl and frame drums, played by the Fatimah Shaddad Musical Ensemble. [Doha, Qatar, 1988]

Drummers and dancers. [Téda people, Chad, Africa, 1970s]

Heating the *tars* to tighten their skins before a performance. [Doha, Qatar, 1988]

Africa

Drum orchestra of a Bantu chief.
[Baule people, Ivory Coast, 1965]

Barrel drum.
[West Africa, date unknown]

Shekere-type calabash rattles. [Baule people, Ivory Coast, mid-1960s]

Likembe. [Luanda region, Angola, date unknown]

Kettledrums on camelback. [Nigeria, 1969]

LISTENING

There are different ways of listening to music. There is a technical state when a person who is developed in technique and has learnt to appreciate better music, feels disturbed by a lower grade of music. But there is a spiritual way, which has nothing to do with technique. It is simply to tune oneself to the music; therefore the spiritual person does not worry about the grade of the music. No doubt, the better the music the more helpful it is to a spiritual person; but at the same time one must not forget there are lamas in Tibet who do their concentrations and meditations while moving a kind of rattle, the sound of which is not specially melodious. They cultivate thereby that sense which raises a person by the help of vibration to the higher planes. There is nothing better than music as a means for the upliftment of the soul. **HAZRAT INAYAT KHAN**

Gourd rattles.
[Burkina Faso, 1974]

Gourd rattle.
[Ashanti people, Ghana, 1971]

Planet Drum

193

Drum, xylophones. [Senufo people, Ivory Coast, 1965]

Dancing with drums. [Senufo people, Ivory Coast, 1965]

Rattling metal disks enrich the sound of drum sets. [Baule people, Ivory Coast, date unknown]

Moropa, earthenware drum. [Sotho people, Orange Free State, South Africa, date unknown]

Log xylophone and drum. [Central Africa, date unknown]

Timbila. [Chopi people, Mozambique, ca. 1935]

Bamboo slit-drums, calabash rattle, buffalo horn beaters. [Dan people, Ivory Coast, 1964]

Mbira (njari-type), **played by Simon Mashoko.** [Harare, Zimbabwe, 1971]

Asia and Oceania

'Au ni mako, struck bamboo tubes.
['Are'Are people, Malaita, Solomon Islands, ca. 1974]

'O'o mouta, played by Warousu.
['Are'Are people, Malaita, Solomon Islands, ca. 1974]

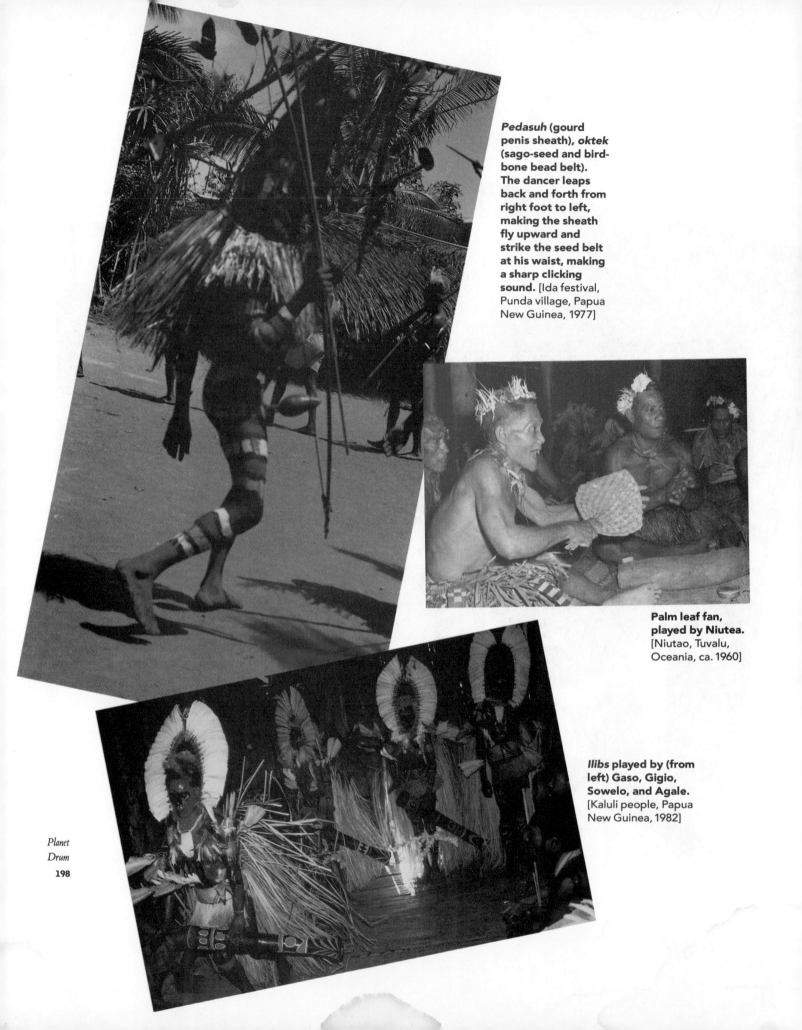

Pedasuh (gourd penis sheath), *oktek* (sago-seed and bird-bone bead belt). The dancer leaps back and forth from right foot to left, making the sheath fly upward and strike the seed belt at his waist, making a sharp clicking sound. [Ida festival, Punda village, Papua New Guinea, 1977]

Palm leaf fan, played by Niutea. [Niutao, Tuvalu, Oceania, ca. 1960]

Ilibs played by (from left) Gaso, Gigio, Sowelo, and Agale. [Kaluli people, Papua New Guinea, 1982]

Kundus. [Arawe plantation, Cape Merkus, New Britain, Papua New Guinea, 1910]

Puks. [South Korea, ca. 1955]

Barrel drums, kettledrums, and *shawm.* [Baltit, Hunza, Pakistan, 1973]

***Rnga*, played by Bhirendra.** [Nepal, 1976] ▼

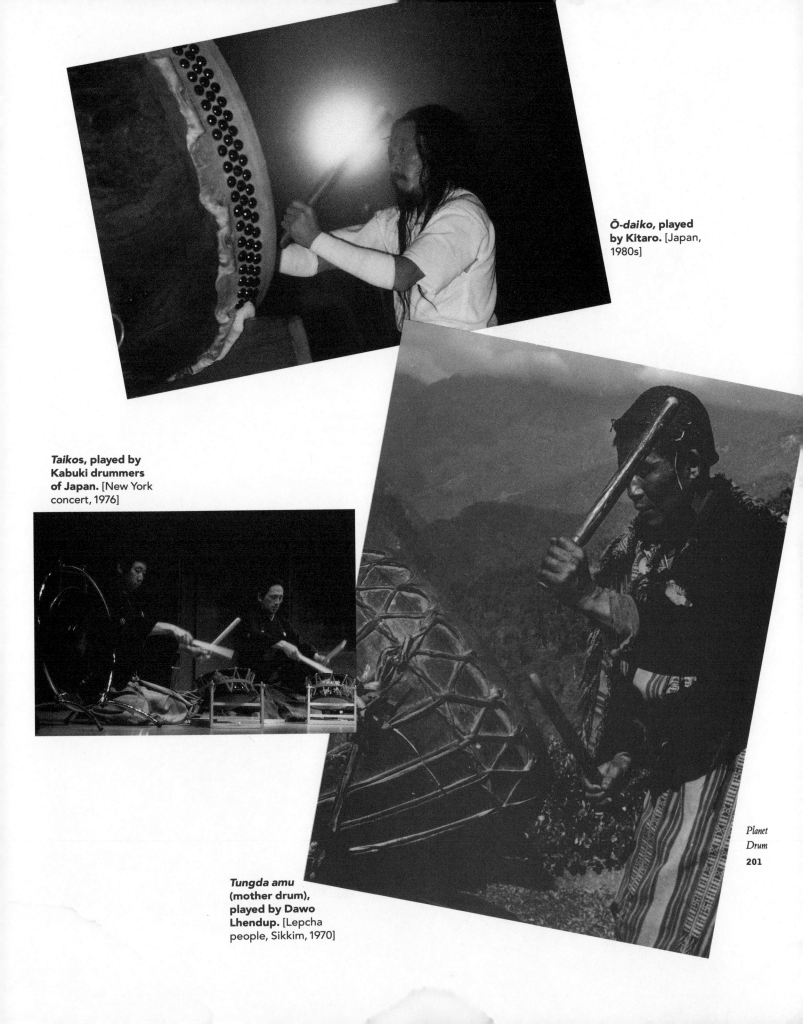

Ō-daiko, played by Kitaro. [Japan, 1980s]

Taikos, played by Kabuki drummers of Japan. [New York concert, 1976]

Tungda amu (mother drum), played by Dawo Lhendup. [Lepcha people, Sikkim, 1970]

Planet Drum

201

There once was a village in Vietnam that was besieged by an army about to attack, but there were no defending soldiers in the village. One bold person assembled a set of nine drums and vigorously performed on all of them, striking rapidly with hands, knees, feet, elbows, shoulders, whatever, making such a din that the attacking troops thought it would be hopeless to go up against the tremendous army that they imagined was there.

FREDRIC LIEBERMAN

Gang-sans with human jawbone handles (left and below). [Bontoc Igorot people, Philippines, 1903]

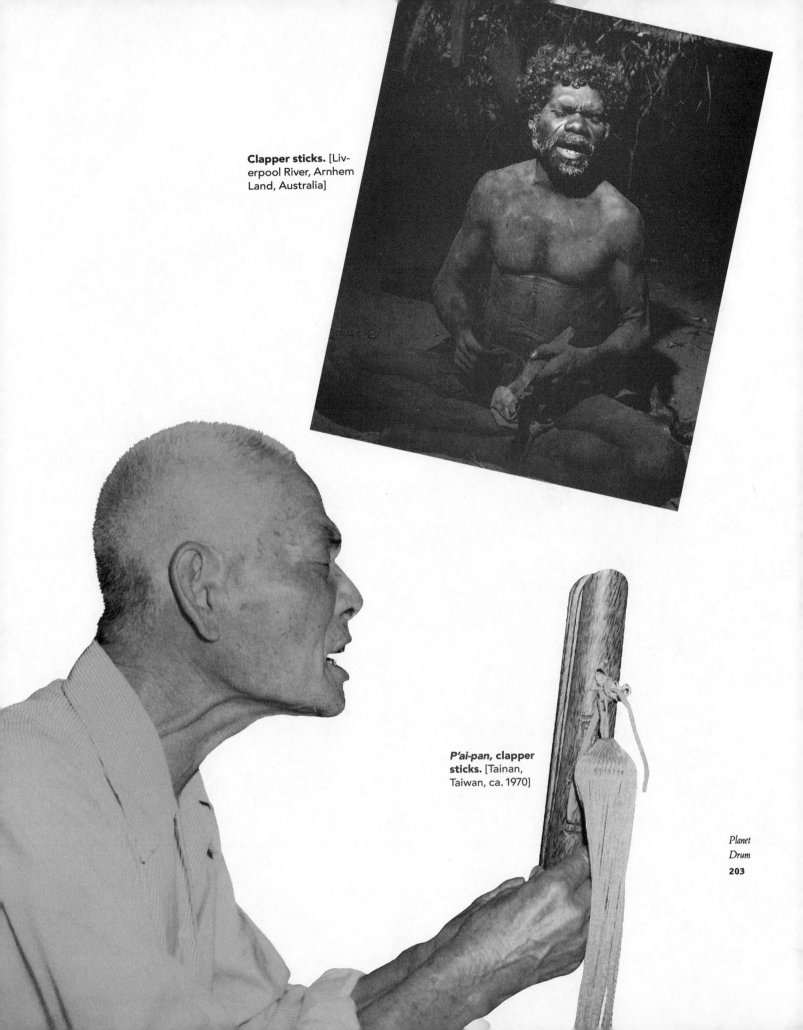

Clapper sticks. [Liverpool River, Arnhem Land, Australia]

P'ai-pan, **clapper sticks.** [Tainan, Taiwan, ca. 1970]

TAIKO

Taiko means "drum" (literally, "big drum") in Japanese. Many different instruments are called *taiko*, including cylindrical and barrel-shaped drums. The *taiko* used in Buddhist and Shinto festivals is usually a large barrel-shaped drum with two nailed heads.

Contemporary *taiko* groups are modeled on the Sado Okesa festivals found only on tiny Sado Island near the Japanese coast. In the 1960s several folkloric ensembles expanded on the Sado Okesa version of *taiko* and created an entirely new style of multiple-drum ensemble music, a style so immediately attractive and exciting that it spread like wildfire across Japan and to Japanese communities overseas.

The best known of these professional ensembles are the Kodo and Ondeko-za drummers. Noted for their rhythmic intensity, these groups treat drumming as if it were a spiritual or martial discipline. Playing in such groups is a highly physical art that focuses all attention on the precision of execution and primacy of the pulse.

Taikos, **played by Kodo.** [Sado Island, Japan, 1980s]

The island archipelago of Indonesia hosts one of the world's richest musical traditions. The gamelan orchestras of Java and Bali are wondrous percussion ensembles composed of gongs, marimba-like metal-keyed instruments, xylophones, drums, and cymbals. Though other instruments are included in gamelan orchestras, bronze is the main sounding material. Try to imagine the sound of an orchestra of bronze — not just the roar of the large gongs or the bright metallic clatter of metal keys, but every possible shade in between, from the purr of low-pitched keys over bamboo resonators struck with heavily padded beaters to the chiming clash of sets of small cymbals.

▲ **Bronze drums are common in southern China and Southeast Asia. Symbols of wealth and power, they still are used in ritual contexts by Shan and Karen peoples.** [Eastern Burma, 1930s]

Kĕndangs. [Bali, Indonesia, 1930s]

Planet Drum

In the many gamelan traditions of the Indonesian archipelago, the musician assigned to the largest gongs plays an essential role by punctuating important structural moments in the music. [Bali, Indonesia, ca. 1930]

Kĕmpur [Bali, Indonesia, 1930s] ▼

In 1893 the Javanese brought a gamelan to Chicago's Columbian Exposition, where the group played to capacity audiences during their six-month run. The instruments languished in storage at Chicago's Field Museum until a perceptive curator recognized their significance, arranged careful restoration, and gave voice to the renewed instruments.

Children

Around the world, thousands of children are living the joy and magic of playing the drum, thrilled by the feeling of stick or hand striking taut drumskin, awed by the clap of sound that fills the ear completely.

Para ni 'o'o. ['Are'Are people, Malaita, Solomon Islands, ca. 1974]

Gamĕlan angklung. [Bali, Indonesia, 1930s] ▶

Gongs. [Bagobo people, Mindanao, Philippines, ca. 1908]

Trap set, played by Buddy Rich. [United States, ca. 1923]

TRAPS
THE DRUM WONDER
USING *Ludwig* DRUMS

***Damaru*, played by Khamtul Rinpoche.** [Khampagar Monastery, Paprola, Himachal Pradesh, India, 1983] ▶

Jacob Armen. [Los Angeles, 1989]

REMO JACOB ARMEN

JACOB ARMEN REMO

***Mridangam*, played by a drum school student.** [Madras, India, 1970]

▲ **Trap set, played by Taro Hart.** [United States, 1986]

***Dholak* and tin box.** [India, ca. 1980]

Planet Drum

From the five-gallon pail to the digitized drum pad, throughout our history as a percussive species we have found endlessly creative ways to turn the world into our drumskin, our hollow log. From the men's and women's drum circles, which are recovering the communal power of entrainment, to the most avant-garde techno-percussionists, we remain time-keepers of an ancient art that harks back to the One, the Nada Brahma, the seed sound at the heart of creation, the big bang. Here are some of the preservers of the pulse.

Five-gallon pail, played by Larry Wright. [United States, 1989]

In this mechanized percussive sculpture, the Earth, under attack by the Rock Thrower and defended by Primitive Squatting Man, splits open to unleash its spirit, the Tumbling Man. The soundscape of the industrialized world is reflected in music. In its image, we create musical instruments, machines that move and dance a very noisy dance. [Chico MacMurtrie, the Exploratorium, San Francisco, 1989]

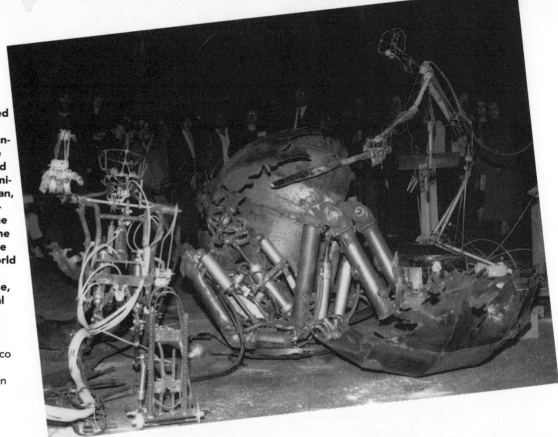

D'Cuckoo is comprised of four electronically digitized percussion instruments played by Tina Phelps, Candice Pacheco, Tina Blaine, and Patti Clemens. [United States, 1991]

Women's drum circle. [Owl and Eagle Lodge, Sebastopol, California, 1991]

Bibliography

Almeida, Bira. *Capoeira: A Brazilian Art Form; History, Philosophy, and Practice.* Berkeley, CA: North Atlantic Books, 1986.

Anoyanakis, Fivos. *Greek Popular Musical Instruments.* Athens: National Bank of Greece, 1979.

Attali, Jacques. *Noise: The Political Economy of Music.* Translated by Brian Massumi. Minneapolis: University of Minnesota Press, 1985.

Bebey, Francis. *African Music: A People's Art.* Translated by Josephine Bennet. New York: Lawrence Hill, 1975.

Belo, Jane. *Trance in Bali.* New York: Columbia University Press, 1960.

———, ed. *Traditional Balinese Culture.* New York: Columbia University Press, 1970.

Blacking, John. *How Musical Is Man?* Seattle: University of Washington Press, 1973.

———. "Dance, Conceptual Thought and Production in the Archaeological Record." In *Problems in Economic and Social Archaeology,* edited by G. de G. Sieveking, I. H. Longworth, and K. E. Wilson. London: Duckworth, 1976.

———. *A Commonsense View of All Music.* Cambridge, England: Cambridge University Press, 1987.

Blades, James. *A Checklist of the Percussion Instruments in the Edinburgh Collection of Historic Musical Instruments.* Edinburgh: Edinburgh University Collection of Historic Musical Instruments, 1982.

———. *Percussion Instruments and Their History.* London: Faber & Faber, 1984.

Blades, James, and Jeremy Montagu. *Early Percussion Instruments from the Middle Ages to the Baroque.* London: Oxford University Press, 1976.

Bragard, Roger, and F. J. de Hen. *Les instruments de musique dans l'art et l'histoire.* Rhode-St-Genese, Belgium: Compagnie Belge d'Editions S.P.R.L., 1967.

Bril, Jacques. *A cordes et à cris: Origines et symbolisme des instruments de musique.* Paris: Éditions Clancier/Guénaud, 1980.

Brincard, Maire-Therese, ed. *Sounding Forms: African Musical Instruments.* New York: American Federation of the Arts, 1989.

Brodzky, Anne T., Rose Danesewich, and Nick Johnson, eds. *Stones, Bones, and Skin: Ritual and Shamanic Art.* Toronto: Society for Art Publications, 1977.

Brown, Howard Mayer, and Joan Lascelle. *Musical Iconography: A Manual for Cataloguing Musical Subjects in Western Art Before 1800.* Cambridge, MA: Harvard University Press, 1972.

Buchner, Alexander. *Musical Instruments through the Ages.* Translated by Iris Urwin. London: Batchworth Press, 1961.

Burke, James. *Connections.* Boston: Little, Brown, 1978.

Cage, John. *Silence.* Middletown, CT: Wesleyan University Press, 1961.

Campbell, Joseph. *The Hero with a Thousand Faces.* 2d ed. Princeton, NJ: Princeton University Press, 1968.

———. *The Masks of God: Primitive Mythology.* New York: Viking Press, 1969.

———. *The Masks of God: Creative Mythology.* New York: Viking Press, 1970.

———. *The Masks of God: Occidental Mythology.* New York: Viking Press, 1970.

———. *The Masks of God: Oriental Mythology.* New York: Viking Press, 1970.

———. *The Mythic Image.* Princeton, NJ: Princeton University Press, 1974.

———. *Historical Atlas of World Mythology, Vol. 1: The Way of the Animal Powers.* New York: Harper & Row, 1983.

———. *Historical Atlas of World Mythology, Vol. 2: The Way of the Seeded Earth, Part 1: The Sacrifice.* New York: Harper & Row, 1988.

Carrington, John F. *Talking Drums of Africa.* New York: Negro Universities Press, 1969.

Chenoweth, Vida. *Musical Instruments of Papua New Guinea.* Port Moresby: Papua New Guinea: Summer Institute of Linguistics, 1976.

Chernoff, John Miller. *African Rhythm and African Sensibility: Aesthetics and Social Action in African Musical Idioms.* Chicago: University of Chicago Press, 1979.

Christensen, Dieter, and Gerd Koch. *Die Musik der Ellice-Inseln.* Berlin: Museum fur Völkerkunde, 1964.

Crossley-Holland, Peter. *Musical Instruments in Tibetan Legend and Folklore.* Los Angeles: University of California Press, 1982.

Crowther, Bruce. *Gene Krupa: His Life and Times.* New York: Universe Books, 1987.

Daniélou, Alain. *Shiva and Dionysus: The Religion of Nature and Eros.* Translated by K. F. Hurry. New York: Inner Traditions International, 1982.

Densmore, Frances. "Music of Santo Domingo Pueblo, New Mexico." In *Southwest Museum Papers #12.* Los Angeles: Southwest Museum, May 1938.

Deren, Maya. *Divine Horsemen: The Living Gods of Haiti.* London: Thames & Hudson, 1953.

Dewey, John. *Art as Experience.* New York: Minton, Balch, 1934.

The Diagram Group. *Musical Instruments of the World: An Illustrated Encyclopedia.* New York: Bantam Books, 1987.

Diallo, Yaya, and Mitchell Hall. *The Healing Drum: African Wisdom Teachings.* Rochester, VT: Destiny Books, 1989.

Dias, Margot. *Instrumentos musicais de mocambique.* Lisbon: Instituto de Investigacao Cientifica Tropical, 1986.

Dioszegi, Vilmos, and M. Hoppal, eds. *Shamanism in Siberia.* Bibliotheca Uralica series, 1. Budapest: Akademiai Kiado, 1978.

Dournon, Geneviève. *Guide for the Collection of Traditional Musical Instruments.* Paris: Unesco Press, 1981.

Dreisbach, Elizabeth. "Change Ringing in England." Master's thesis in Ethnomusicology, University of Washington, 1983.

Eichenberg, Fritz. *Dance of Death: A Graphic Commentary on the Danse Macabre through the Centuries.* New York: Abbeville Press, ca. 1983.

Eliade, Mircea. *Birth and Rebirth: The Religious Meanings of Initiation in Human Culture.* Translated by Willard R. Trask. New York: Harper & Row, 1958.

———. *Shamanism: Archaic Techniques of Ecstasy.* Translated by Willard R. Trask. Princeton, NJ: Princeton University Press, 1972.

Emsheimer, Ernst. *Studia ethnomusicologica Eurasiatica.* Stockholm: Musikhistoriska Museet, 1964.

Farmer, Henry George. *The Rise and Development of Military Music.* London: Reeves, 1912.

———. *Military Music.* New York: Chanticleer Press, 1950.

Feld, Steven. *Sound and Sentiment: Birds, Weeping, Poetics, and Song in Kaluli Expression.* Philadelphia: University of Pennsylvania Press, 1982. 2d ed., 1990.

Fischer, Hans. *Sound-Producing Instruments in Oceania: Construction and Playing Technique — Distribution and Function.* Translated by Philip W. Holzknecht. Port Moresby: Papua New Guinea: Institute of Papua New Guinea Studies, 1983.

Fitzhugh, William W., and Aron Crowell. *Crossroads of Continents: Cultures of Siberia and Alaska.* London: Smithsonian Institution Press, 1988.

Fraser, J. T. *Of Time, Passion, and Knowledge: Reflections on the Strategy of Existence.* New York: George Braziller, 1975.

Gansemans, Jos. *Les instruments de musique Luba (Shaba, Zaire).* Tervuren, Belgium: Koninklijk Museum Voor Midden-Afrika, 1980.

Gimbutas, Marija. *The Language of the Goddess.* San Francisco: Harper & Row, 1989.

Godwin, Joscelyn. *Athanasius Kircher: A Renaissance Man and the Quest for Lost Knowledge.* London: Thames & Hudson, 1979.

Gowan, John Curtis. *Trance, Art, and Creativity.* Northridge, CA: California State University, 1975.

Guaman Poma de Ayala, Felipe. *Nueva coronica y buen gobierno.* Paris: Institut d'Ethnologie, 1936.

Guru Rinpoche, according to Karma Lingpa. *The Tibetan Book of the Dead: The Great Liberation through Hearing in the Bardo.* Translated by Francesca Fremantle and Chogyam Trungpa. Boston: Shambhala, 1987.

Halifax, Joan. *Shaman: The Wounded Healer.* New York: Crossroad, 1982.

Harter, Jim, ed. *Music: A Pictorial Archive of Woodcuts and Engravings.* New York: Dover, 1980.

Hazen, Margaret H., and Robert M. Hazen. *The Music Men: An Illustrated History of Brass Bands in America, 1800–1920.* Washington, DC: Smithsonian Institution Press, 1987.

Herskovits, Melville J. *The Myth of the Negro Past.* Boston: Beacon Press, 1958.

Hickmann, Hans. *45 siècles de musique dans L'Egypte ancienne: A travers la sculpture, la peinture, l'instrument.* Paris: Editions Richard-Masse, 1956.

Hood, Mantle. *The Ethnomusicologist.* New York: McGraw-Hill, 1971. Kent, OH: Kent State University Press, 1982.

Hornbostel, E. M. von. "The Ethnology of African Sound-Instruments: Comments on Gest und Werden der Musik-Instrumente by C. Sachs." *Africa: Journal of the International Institute of African Languages and Cultures* 6 (April, 1933).

Horniman Museum. *Musical Instruments.* London: London County Council, 1958.

Hsu, Dolores M., ed. *The Henry Eichheim Collection of Oriental Instruments: A Western Musician Discovers a New World of Sound.* Santa Barbara: University Art Museum, 1984.

Hyslop, Graham. *Musical Instruments of East Africa, One: Kenya.* Nairobi: Nelson, 1975.

Inayat Khan, Hazrat. *The Sufi Message of Hazrat Inayat Khan, Vol. 2: Music.* London: Barrie & Jenkins, 1973.

Janata, Alfred. *Musikinstrumente der Volker: Außereuropaische Musikinstrumente und Schallgeräte: Systematik und Themenbeispiele.* Vienna: Museum für Volkerkunde, 1975.

Jones, A. M. *Africa and Indonesia: The Evidence of the Xylophone and Other Musical and Cultural Factors.* Leiden, Netherlands: E. J. Brill, 1964.

Jung, Carl G. *Man and His Symbols.* New York: Doubleday, 1964.

Kandell, Alice S., and Charlotte Y. Salisbury. *Mountaintop Kingdom: Sikkim.* New York: Norton, 1971.

King, Anthony. *Yoruba Sacred Music from Ekiti.* Ibadan, Nigeria: Ibadan University Press, 1961.

Kirby, Percival R. *The Musical Instruments of the Native Races of South Africa.* Johannesburg: Witwatersrand University Press, 1965.

Krakatoa Committee of the Royal Society. *The Eruption of Krakatoa,* London: Royal Society, 1888.

Kuttner, Fritz A. *The Archaeology of Ancient Chinese Music.* New York: Paragon, 1990.

Langer, Susanne K. *Philosophical Sketches.* Baltimore: Johns Hopkins Press, 1962.

Lomax, Alan. *Folk Song Style and Culture.* Washington, DC: American Association for the Advancement of Science, 1968.

Mensink, Onno, ed. *Japanese Woodcuts with Music.* Büren, West Germany: Haags Gemeentemuseum and Frits Knuf, 1975.

Merriam, Alan P. *The Anthropology of Music.* Chicago: Northwestern University Press, 1964.

Mersenne, Marin. *Harmonie Universelle: The Books on Instruments.* Translated by Roger E. Chapman. The Hague: Nijhoff, 1957.

Metropolitan Museum of Art. *Musical Instruments in the Metropolitan Museum.* New York: Metropolitan Museum of Art, 1978.

Meyer-Baer, Kathi. *Music of the Spheres and the Dance of Death: Studies in Musical Iconology.* Princeton, NJ: Princeton University Press, 1970.

Montesinos, Fernando. *Memorias antiguas historiales del Peru.* Translated and edited by Philip Ainsworth Means, with an introduction by Sir Clements R. Markham. London: Hakluyt Society, 1920.

Murdock, George Peter. *Africa: Its Peoples and Their Cultural History.* New York: McGraw-Hill, 1959.

———. *Behavior Science Outlines, Vol. 1: Outline of Cultural Materials.* 4th rev. ed. New Haven, CT: Human Relations Area Files, 1965.

———. *Outline of World Cultures.* 5th ed. New Haven, CT: Human Relations Area Files, 1975.

Music Educators National Conference. *Music Educators Journal* 59 (October 1972).

Nadel, Siegfried. "The Origins of Music." *Musical Quarterly* 16 (1936): 531–546.

National Geographic Book Service. *The World of the American Indian.* Washington, DC: National Geographic Society, 1989.

Needham, Rodney. "Percussion and Transition." In *Reader in Comparative Religion: An Anthropological Approach,* edited by William A. Lessa and Evan Z. Vogt. 3d ed. New York: Harper & Row, 1972.

Neher, Andrew. "A Physiological Explanation of Unusual Behavior in Ceremonies Involving Drums." *Human Biology* 34 (1962): 151–160.

Nettl, Bruno. *The Study of Ethnomusicology: Twenty-nine Issues and Concepts.* Urbana: University of Illinois Press, 1983.

Partch, Harry. *Genesis of a Music: An Account of a Creative Work, Its Roots and Its Fulfillments.* New York: Da Capo Press, 1974.

Pauline, Mark, and Matt Heckert. *Survival Research Laboratories: 23 Photographs of Machinery and Performances.* San Francisco: Visible Spectrum, 1988.

Picken, Laurence E. R. *Folk Musical Instruments of Turkey.* London: Oxford University Press, 1975.

Praetorius, Michael. *Syntagma musicum. II, De organographia: Parts I and II.* Translated and edited by David Z. Crookes. Oxford: Clarendon Press, 1986.

Price, Percival. *Bells and Man.* Oxford: Oxford University Press, 1983

Reck, David. *Music of the Whole Earth.* New York: Scribner's, 1977.

Redmond, Layne. "Rhythm and the Frame Drum: Attributes of the Goddess." *Ear, Magazine of New Music* 15 (June, 1990): 18–21.

Rimmer, Joan. *Ancient Musical Instruments of Western Asia: In the Department of Western Asiatic Antiquities, the British Museum.* London: British Musem, 1969.

Rouget, Gilbert. *Music and Trance: A Theory of the Relations between Music and Possession.* Chicago: University of Chicago Press, 1985.

Rubtsov, N. N. *History of Foundry Practice in the USSR.* New Delhi: Indian National Scientific Documentation Centre, 1975.

Russolo, Luigi. *The Art of Noises.* Translated by Barclay Brown. New York: Pendragon Press, 1986.

Sachs, Curt. *The History of Musical Instruments.* New York: Norton, 1940.

———. *The Rise of Music in the Ancient World, East and West.* New York: Norton, 1943.

———. *Rhythm and Tempo: A Study in Music History.* New York: Norton, 1953.

———. *World History of the Dance.* Translated by Bessie Schonberg. New York: Seven Arts Publishers, 1952.

———. *The Wellsprings of Music.* The Hague: Nijhoff, 1962.

Sagan, Carl. *Cosmos.* New York: Random House, 1980.

Schaeffner, André. *Origine des instruments de musique.* Paris, 1936. New York: Johnson Reprint Corporation, 1968.

Schafer, R. Murray. *The Tuning of the World.* New York: Knopf, 1977.

Seebass, Tilman, ed. *Imago Musicae* (Vols. 1–6). Kassel, West Germany: Bärenreiter-Verlag, 1984–present.

Snellgrove, David, and Hugh Richardson. *A Cultural History of Tibet.* New York: Praeger, 1968.

Spear, Nathaniel, Jr. *A Treasury of Archaeological Bells.* New York: Hastings House, 1978.

Stevenson, Robert. *Music in Aztec and Inca Territory.* Berkeley: University of California Press, 1968.

Sullivan, Lawrence E. *Icanchu's Drum: An Orientation to Meaning in South American Religions.* New York: Macmillan, 1988.

Taylor, Rogan P. *The Death and Resurrection Show: From Shaman to Superstar.* London: Anthony Blond, 1985.

Truslev, Rev. John. *The Works of William Hogarth, in a Series of One Hundred and Fifty Steel Engravings, by the First Artists: With Description and a Comment on Their Moral Tendency . . . To Which are Added, Anecdotes of the Author and His Works, by J. Hogarth and J. Nichols,* Vol. 1. London: London Printing and Publishing Company, 1833.

Vennum, Thomas, Jr. *The Ojibwa Dance Drum: Its History and Construction.* Washington: Smithsonian Institution Press, 1982.

Ventura, Michael. *Shadow Dancing in the U.S.A.* Los Angeles: Tarcher, 1985.

von Franz, Marie-Louise. *Time: Rhythm and Repose.* London: Thames & Hudson, 1978.

Williams, Edward V. *The Bells of Russia: History and Technology.* Princeton, NJ: Princeton University Press, 1985.

Winternitz, Emanuel. *Musical Instruments and Their Symbolism in Western Art.* New York: Norton, 1967.

———. *Leonardo da Vinci as a Musician.* New Haven, CT: Yale University Press, 1982.

Young, Phillip T. *The Look of Music: Rare Musical Instruments, 1500–1900.* Vancouver, Canada: Douglas & McIntyre, 1980.

Zemp, Hugo. *Musique Dan: La Musique dans la pensée et la vie sociale d'une societé africaine.* Paris: Mouton & Co., and École Pratique des Hautes Études, 1971.

Zemp, Hugo, and Daniel de Coppet. *'Are' are: Un peuple melanésien et sa musique.* Paris: Editions du Seuil, 1978.

Discography

The World, a series of recordings produced by Mickey Hart, presents authentic and fusion music from diverse nations and styles, selected for its beauty, power, and significance and recorded in locations ranging from the Nubian Desert to the Arctic Tundra. (For more information about this series, write to: Rykodisc, Pickering Wharf, Bldg. C–3G, Salem, MA 01970.)

The Diga Rhythm Band. *Diga* (RCD 10101/RALP/RACS). Classic percussion from a band of eleven rhythmists, including Mickey Hart and Zakir Hussain, and featuring Jerry Garcia.

Hamza el Din. *Eclipse* (RCD 10103/RACS). Music from the *oud* master from the Sudan.

Dzintars. *Songs of Amber* (RCD 10130/RACS). Folk songs from the Latvian Women's Choir.

Steven Feld, producer. *Voices of the Rainforest* (RCD 10173/RACS). The endangered music of the Kaluli, recorded in Papua New Guinea.

The Golden Gate Gypsy Orchestra. *The Traveling Jewish Wedding* (RCD 10105/RACS). A joyous blend of traditional and contemporary music.

The Gyuto Monks. *Freedom Chants from the Roof of the World* (RCD 20113/RACS). The polyphonic chanting of the Tibetan choir, featuring a performance by Mickey Hart, Philip Glass, and Kitaro.

Hariprasad Chaurasia and Zakir Hussain. *Venu* (RCD 20128). Classical flute music from India, featuring *tabla* master Zakir Hussain.

Mickey Hart. *At the Edge* (RCD 10124/RACS). The companion album to *Drumming at the Edge of Magic,* a personal anthology of Mickey Hart's lifelong pursuit of the spirit of percussion.

————. *Planet Drum* (RCD 10206/RACS). Percussionists from many traditions find common ground to create a dynamic new global style, featuring Sikiru Adepoju, Mickey Hart, Zakir Hussain, Airto Moreira, Babatunde Olatunji, Flora Purim, and T. H. "Vikku" Vinayakram.

Mickey Hart and Taro Hart. *Music to Be Born By* (RCD 20112/RACS). A soothing, rhythmic soundscape for the birthing environment and beyond, featuring a recording of Taro Hart's heartbeat in the womb.

Mickey Hart, Airto Moreira, and Flora Purim. *Dāfos* (RCD 10108/RACS). A musical ethnography of an imaginary country; the adventure of an inner soundscape.

Mickey Hart, producer. *The Music of Upper and Lower Egypt* (RCD 10106/RACS). Recorded during the Grateful Dead's 1978 tour of Egypt.

Ustad Sultan Khan. *Sarangi: The Music of India* (RCD 10104/RACS). The exquisite sounds of the *sarangi.*

Olatunji. *Drums of Passion: The Invocation* (RCD 10102/RACS). A new digital recording by a drum master, featuring eleven percussionists and seven vocalists.

Olatunji. *Drums of Passion: The Beat* (RCD 10107/RACS). A digitally remixed version of *Dance to the Beat of My Drum.*

The Rhythm Devils. *The Apocalypse Now Sessions* (RCD 10109/RACS). Mickey Hart, Bill Kreutzmann, Michael Hinton, and Airto Moreira explore the boundaries of cinematic music.

Thomas Vennum, Jr., and Mickey Hart, producers. *Honor the Earth* (RCD 10199/RACS). A powwow dance ceremony of three American Indian tribes, the Ojibwa, the Menominee, and the Winnebago, recorded in northern Wisconsin.

The Planet Drum ensemble. *Top:* **Flora Purim, Sikiru Adepoju, Mickey Hart, Babatunde Olatunji, Airto Moreira.** *Bottom:* **T. H. "Vikku" Vinayakram, Zakir Hussain.** [United States, 1991]

Acknowledgments

Bira Almeida
Remo Belli
Peter Berg
John Blacking
Barry Brook
Carol and Joe Calato
Joseph Campbell
George Carroll
Barton Cline
Elizabeth Cohen
Nina Cummings
Vince Delgado
Sue Carole De Vale
Lennie DiMuzio
Rick Drumm
Alan Dundes
Catherine Dunford
Leah Farrow
Steven Feld
Vic Firth
Jerry Garcia
Robert Garfias
Sara De Gennaro
Samuel M. Goldberger
Thomas Grady
Marilyn Graf
Bill Graham
The Grateful Dead
Grateful Dead
   Productions staff
David Gregory
Lou Harrison
Creek Hart
Taro Hart
Marty Hartmann
Bess Hawes
Sheryl Heidenreich
Ruth-Inge Heinze
Michael Hinton
Mantle Hood
Dolores Hsu
Naut Humon
Robert Hunter
Zakir Hussain

Howard Jacobsen
Jung Institute of San
   Francisco
Mariko Kan
Bryna Kan-Lieberman
Richard Keeling
Charlie King
Stacy Kluck
Roderic Knight
Kodo
Stanley Krippner
Fritz Kuttner
Dennis Letzler
Emily Levy
Horst Link
Maury Lishon
Alan Lomax
José Lorenzo
William F. Ludwig
James Makubuye
Dr. Alan Margolin
Lloyd McCausland
Barbara McClintock
Nion McEvoy
Dennis McNally
Charles McNamee
Patricia McNamee
Susan McNamee
Barry Melton
Antonia Minnecola
Gyuto Monks
Ken Moore
Airto Moreira
Bill Morgan
Gordon Mumma
Keith Muscutt
Andy Narrell

Andrew Neher
New York General
   Library of
   Performing Arts
New York Public
   Library
Babatunde Olatunji
Constance Olds
James Olnes
Mark Pauline
Michael Pluznick
Jerry Pompili
Tito Puente
Flora Purim
Barbara Racy
Jihad Racy
Regal Tip
Sabian Ltd.
Andrew Schloss
Cameron Sears
Pete Seeger
Guha Shankar
Dan Sheehy
Robert Sheldon
Ram Rod Shurtliff
The Smithsonian
   Institution
Susan Sommer
Jay Stevens
Daphne Thompson
Tovar Vanderbeek
Lois Vanderbeek
Thomas Vennum, Jr.
Jesse Virago
Gillian Wakely
Bob Ward
Diane Alexander
   White
Connie Whitman
Kay Wolverton
Wordata

Hugo Zemp
Armand Zildjian
Avedis Zildjian Co.
Robert Zildjian

**HARPER
SAN FRANCISCO
STAFF**

Pamela Byers
Clayton Carlson
Ani Chamichian
Jim McCasland
Adrian Morgan
Noreen Norton
Pat Rose
Bernie Scheier
Robin Seaman

**TRIAD
STAFF AND
ASSOCIATES**

Robin Benjamin
Stuart Bradford
Michael Dambrowski
Roger Graham
Ariel Grey
Janet Huston
Jon Ianziti
Dagmar Jordan
Nancy Kivette
Jean Lannen
David Meyer
Jerry Pisani
Cindi Powers
Evelyn Reece
Michelle Rose
Inga Vesik

**ARTISTS AND
ILLUSTRATORS**

David Beck
Maya Cain
Kalynn Campbell
David Delamare
Carol Lavelle

RESEARCHERS

Francesca Ferguson
Michael Frishkopf
Jennie Hansen
Kathryn Henniss
Mei-lu Ho
Louise Lacey
Ted Levitt
Therese Mahoney
John O'Connell
Patrizia Pallaro
David Phillips
David Roche
Nicholas Sammond
Richard Sheiman
Curt L. Sonneborn
Elizabeth Wright

**360°
PRODUCTIONS
STAFF**

Dante Anderson
Howard Cohen
Christine Coulter
Nance Dunev
Mark Forry
Janey Fritsche
Shannon Hamilton
Edith Johnson
Steve Keyser
Leslie Michel
Merri Parker
Michael Peri
John Perdikis
Sheila Smith
Jeff Sterling
Karen Tautenhahn
Lori Zook

CREDITS

COVER ILLUSTRATION: Nancy Nimoy; animal spirits concept courtesy of Willard H. Dow II. **INITIAL CAPS:** David Beck. **8–9:** © Gary Ladd 1972. **11:** Finley Holiday Film, Los Angeles. **12:** Ullstein-Bilderdienst; National Aeronautics and Space Administration, Washington, D.C. **13:** Original illustration by Educational Event Coordinators, San Francisco, after *Man the Toolmaker,* 5th edition, by K. P. Oakley (London: British Museum, 1958); L. Patrignani, Arti Grafiche Ricordi, Milan, Italy. **14:** Original illustration by Kalynn Campbell. **15:** Peter Veit, © National Geographic Society. **16:** Norton Simon Foundation. **17:** Courtesy of Silvio A. Bedini, Smithsonian Institution. **18:** The British Library. **19:** © The Pierpont Morgan Library 1990. **21:** Original illustration by David Delamare. **22:** Original illustration by Kalynn Campbell. **24:** Original illustration by David Delamare. **27:** Original illustration by Educational Event Coordinators, San Francisco. **28:** Original illustration by David Delamare. **30:** Jean Vertut. **31:** Landesmuseum für Vorgeschichte (t); Cooperation (mr); Neg. no. 330490, Courtesy of the Department of Library Services, American Museum of Natural History (b). **32:** Reproduced by courtesy of the Trustees of the British Museum (tl); Reproduced by courtesy of the Trustees of the British Museum (crotales); Hirmer Fotoarchiv, Munich (b). **33:** Reproduced by courtesy of the Trustees of the British Museum (tl); Reproduced by courtesy of the Trustees of the British Museum (tr); Courtesy

of the Egyptian Museum, Cairo (CG69220 A,B) (mr); Courtesy of the Egyptian Museum, Cairo (CG40015) (br); Reproduced by courtesy of the Trustees of the British Museum (bl). **34:** Wang Mengxiang, courtesy of Pan Qixu (tl); Courtesy of the Royal Ontario Museum, Toronto, Canada (mr); From *Heavenly Clockwork: The Great Astronomical Clocks of Medieval China,* by Joseph Needham (Cambridge: Cambridge University Press, 1960) (br). **35:** Chinese Culture Center (drumsinger). **36:** By permission of the Syndics of Cambridge University Library (tr); Bardo Museum, Tunis (bl). **37:** F. Anton, Munich (tl); Lowie Museum of Anthropology, The University of California at Berkeley (tc); Photograph by F. Anton, from the collection of Howard Leigh, Museo Frissil, Mitla, Oaxaca, Mexico (tr); F. Anton (c); INAH·CNCA·MEX (b). **38:** The Heard Museum, Phoenix, Arizona; Carmelo Guadagno, courtesy of Museum of the American Indian, Heye Foundation. **39:** Reproduction courtesy of The Bancroft Library (tl); Arizona State Museum, The University of Arizona, photograph by Helga Teiwes (tr); F. Anton, Munich. **40:** © 1990, Museo del Prado, Madrid, Spain. **41:** Wallraf-Richartz-Museum, Köln, photograph by Rheinische Bildarchiv. **42:** From *The Works of William Hogarth* (London: London Printing and Publishing Co., 1833); Joseph Glanville, *Saducismus Triumphatus,* courtesy of the Huntington Library, San Marino, California; *Oeuvre Lithographié de Honoré Daumier* (Paris: Loys Delteil, 1925). **43:** Reproduced from the *Oxford English Dictionary* by permission of Oxford University Press (background); From *Russolo: l'Arte dei Rumori* by G. Franco Maffina (Torino: Martano/Vias Battista, 1978). **44:** From *Newsweek,* August 8, 1936 (tr); International Museum of Photography at George Eastman House, photograph by Lewis Hine (tl); Thomas Erikson (bl); Vince Maggiora, courtesy of *San Francisco Chronicle* (demolition). **45:** United States Navy Flight Demonstration Squadron, Pensacola, Florida, photograph by Jeff Wood (tr); United States Navy Flight Demonstration Squadron, Pensacola, Florida,

photograph by Jeff Wood (mr); Ullstein-Bilderdienst, photograph by Pavel Sticha (c). **46–47:** Isao Suto. **49:** Biblioteka Kornicka PAN. **50:** From *Greek Folk Musical Instruments,* by Fivos Anoyanakis (Athens: National Bank of Greece, 1979), pl. 19, photograph by K. Paschalidis. **51:** Hugo Zemp. **52:** Vidoc, department of the Royal Tropical Institute, Amsterdam, Netherlands. **53:** From *Talking Drums of Africa,* by John F. Carrington (New York: Negro Universities Press, 1969). **54:** Mantle Hood; Hugo Zemp. **55:** Drawing by Chas. Addams, © 1986 The New Yorker Magazine, Inc. (tl); Courtesy, Field Museum of Natural History (neg. no. 100851), Chicago (tr); © 1927 Metro-Goldwyn-Mayer Distributing Corporation, ren. 1955 Loew's Inc. (br). **56–57:** Edinburgh University Library Or. Ms. 20, folio 108v. **57:** Burgerbibliothek, Bern. **58:** Courtesy of Topkapi Sarayi Museum; Glasgow University Library, Farmer Collection (Farmer Mss. 126/2). **59:** Musées Royaux des Beaux-Arts de Belgique, Brussels, photograph by Speltdoorn. **60:** Reproduced by courtesy of the Trustees of the British Museum. **61:** Detail from the Battle of Blenheim Tapestry, reproduced by kind permission of His Grace the Duke of Marlborough; Plymouth City Museum & Art Gallery Collection, England. **62:** Delaware Art Museum, Wilmington, Howard Pyle Collection; The Fotomas Index. **63:** From *Drummer's Heritage,* by Frederick Fennel, courtesy of Ludwig Music. **64:** Mezzotint in the Farmer Collection, Glasgow University Library; Royal Military School of Music, Kneller Hall, Twickenham, England. **65:** Ronn Palm; Attributed to Matthew Brady, courtesy of William Ludwig Archive. **66:** William Ludwig Archive; Amon Carter Museum, Fort Worth, Texas. **67:** From *The Illustrated London News,* August 5, 1876; *Scientific American* Supplement, September 1900. **68:** Original illustration by David Beck. **70:** Neg. no. 322202, photograph by Bottin, courtesy of Department of Library Services, American Museum of Natural History. **71:** Stedelijk Museum Collection, Amsterdam, © Estate of George Grosz/VAGA New

York 1990. **72:** United States Department of Energy, 1957. **73:** From *A Pictorial History of the SS: 1923–1945,* by Andrew Mollo (London: Macdonald & Jane's Publishing Group) (tl); From *Hitler's Propaganda Machine,* by Ward Rutherford (London: Bison Books) (tr); Yad Vashem Photo Archives (b). **74:** Eberhard Otto. **75:** Chicago Historical Society, photograph by H. A. Atwell Studio, ICHi-21729. **76:** Courtesy of Peabody Museum, Harvard University. **77:** Hugo Zemp; Reprinted from *Music Educators Journal,* October 1972 (vol. 59, no. 2). **78:** The Laura Boulton Collection, Archives of Traditional Music, Indiana University. **79:** Courtesy of Colin McPhee Collection, UCLA Ethnomusicology Archive; Steven Feld. **80:** *Ichimura actor in the role of street musician,* by Katsukawa Shunko, Collection Haags Gemeentemuseum, The Hague; The Metropolitan Museum of Art, Charles Stewart Smith Collection, gift of Mrs. Charles Stewart Smith, Charles Stewart Smith, Jr., and Howard Caswell Smith, in memory of Charles Stewart Smith, 1914 (14.76.60.11), all rights reserved, The Metropolitan Museum of Art. **81:** "A Dancing Boy" by Kim Hong-Do (? – after 1814), National Museum of Korea, Seoul (tr); Japan National Tourist Organization (bl). **82:** © 1990 The Metropolitan Museum of Art, purchase, Louis E. and Theresa S. Seley Purchase Fund for Islamic Art, Rogers Fund and Alastair B. Martin, Margaret Mushkian, and Time-Life, Inc. Gifts, 1985 (1985.247); Courtesy of the Trustees of the Victoria and Albert Museum. **83:** Susan Griggs Agency, photograph by Pepita Fairfax (tl); Eliot Elisofon, National Museum of African Art, Eliot Elisofon Archives, Smithsonian Institution (c); Branson De Cou, *National Geographic,* December 1932 (tin cans); John Werner (background). **84:** Courtesy of Topkapi Sarayi Museum; Barbara Racy. **85:** From *Music: A Pictorial Archive of Woodcuts and Engravings,* selected by Jim Harter (New York: Dover Publications Inc., 1980); Barbara Racy. **86:** Carol Beck and Angela Fisher. **87:** Courtesy of the New York Public Library; From *The Illustrated London News,* May 27, 1865.

88: Eliot Elisofon, National Museum of African Art, Eliot Elisofon Archives, Smithsonian Institution. **89:** John Chernoff. **90:** From *Montagnes de la Lune: Documents Photographiques en Noir et en Couleurs,* by Bernard Pierre, Jean-Paul Gardiner, and Bernard Pierre (Paris: Hachette, 1959) (tl); René Gardi (bl). **91:** Carol Beck and Angela Fisher; Eliot Elisofon, National Museum of African Art, Eliot Elisofon Archives, Smithsonian Institution. **92:** Eliot Elisofon, National Museum of African Art, Eliot Elisofon Archives, Smithsonian Institution. **93:** A.A.A. Photo, Paris (tr); Eliot Elisofon, National Museum of African Art, Eliot Elisofon Archives, Smithsonian Institution (ml); United Nations (b). **94:** Courtesy of Biblioteka Narodowa, Warsaw, Poland (tl); Bibliothèque Nationale de Paris (tr). **95:** Reproduced by courtesy of the Trustees of The National Gallery, London (t); O. Wyß-Dierks (br). **96:** Organization of American States; Organization of American States. **97:** Courtesy of Milwaukee Public Museum (tr); Vidoc, department of the Royal Tropical Institute, Amsterdam, Netherlands (tl); Hugh Davis, © 1940 National Geographic Society (b). **98:** Courtesy of Carybé (tl); Courtesy of Carybé (br); Courtesy of Carybé (bl). **99:** Trans. no. 1734(2), courtesy Department of Library Services, American Museum of Natural History; National Anthropological Archives, Smithsonian Institution. **100–1:** Turkish Ministry of Tourism and Information. **103:** © 1990 The Metropolitan Museum of Art, Rogers Fund, 1922 (22.139.28); From *Auserlesene Griechische Vasenbilder,* by Eduard Gerhard (Berlin: G. Reimer, 1843), pl. 115. **104:** From *Altes Musikinstrumentes,* by Wilhelm Stauder (Braunschweig: Klinkhardt & Biermann, 1973) (background); The Metropolitan Museum of Art, Fletcher Fund, 1940 (41.96), all rights reserved, The Metropolitan Museum of Art (bl); Collection, The Museum of Modern Art, New York, acquired through the Lillie P. Bliss Bequest, etching and aquatint, printed in black, pl. 26¼ × 20⅛ in. **105:** Courtesy of Biblioteka

Narodowa, Warsaw, Poland; Fabrizio Parisio. **106:** Stifts, bibliothek, St. Gallen (tr); Fausto Castraberte, Perugia, Italy. **107:** Museum Boymans,van Beuningen, Rotterdam. **108:** Photo Vatican Museums. **109:** From *The Illustrated London News,* November 9, 1878; From *Greek Folk Musical Instruments,* by Fivos Anoyanakis (Athens: National Bank of Greece, 1979), pl. 11, photograph by M. Skiadaressis. **110:** Adam Clark Vroman, National Anthropological Archives, Smithsonian Institution (bl). **111:** Hugo Zemp (tr); Courtesy of Field Museum of Natural History (neg. no. 37934), Chicago (b). **112:** Dance Collection, New York Public Library at Lincoln Center, Astor, Lenox, and Tilden Foundations; Reproduced by courtesy of the Trustees of the British Museum. **113:** B,23638 "Noblewoman," Hans Holbein, the Younger, 1497–1543, National Gallery of Art, Washington, D.C., Rosenwald Collection (tl); B,7438 "End of Mankind," Hans Holbein, the Younger, 1497–1543, National Gallery of Art, Washington, D.C., Rosenwald Collection (tr); Fowler Museum of Cultural History, UCLA (bl). **114:** Stuart Wasserman; Hermann Trenkle. **115:** © 1990 Museo del Prado, Madrid, Spain; Bernisches Historisches Museum. **116:** Courtesy of Field Museum of Natural History (neg. no. 111407C), Chicago; Collection Musée de l'Homme. **117:** Hugo Zemp. **118:** J. Pascal Sébah (after 1868), *Cairo: Fête du Dosseh,* courtesy of the Brooklyn Museum. **119:** © 1980 The Metropolitan Museum of Art, purchase, Rogers Fund and the Kevorkian Foundation Gift, 1955 (55.121.10.18). **120:** Barbara Racy (ml); Lillian Schoedler, *National Geographic,* April 1931 (mr). **121:** Jane Belo; Jane Belo. **122:** Michael Yamashita. **123:** David Lewiston. **124:** Alice Kandell; Alice Kandell. **125:** Staatliche Museum für Völkerkunde. **126:** Archives N. Bouvier. **127:** John Hitchcock. **128:** From *Finno, Ugric, Siberian Mythology,* by Uno Holmberg (New York: Cooper Square, 1964); Larry G. Peters, Ph.D. **129:** Courtesy of Peabody Museum, Harvard University, photograph by Edward Curtis.

130: Barbara Racy. **131:** Matilda Coxe Stevenson, National Anthropological Archives, Smithsonian Institution; National Anthropological Archives, Smithsonian Institution. **132:** From *Reise in das innere Nord, America in den Jahren 1832–1834,* by Prince Maximilian, courtesy of The Bancroft Library. **133:** Rafael José de Menezes Bastos, 1976, courtesy of Gerard Béhague (tr); Peter T. Furst (c); Paintings by Edwin Earle, courtesy of Museum of the American Indian, Heye Foundation (b). **134:** The British Library. **137:** Original illustration by Carol Lavelle. **138:** © D. Laine,Hoa,Qui. **139:** Cherel Ito. **140:** Don Klein; Don Klein. **141:** Don Klein; Don Klein. **142:** From *The Illustrated London News,* May 5, 1888; Don Klein. **143:** Don Klein. **144–45:** Michael Melford. **147:** Remo Inc., Hollywood, California. **148:** Axel Poignant Archive, London; From *Music: A Pictorial Archive of Woodcuts and Engravings,* selected by Jim Harter (New York: Dover Publications Inc., 1980). **149:** From *Greek Folk Musical Instruments,* by Fivos Anoyanakis (Athens: National Bank of Greece, 1979), pl. 48, photograph by R. Parissis (tl); From *Greek Folk Musical Instruments,* by Fivos Anoyanakis (Athens: National Bank of Greece, 1979), pl. 47, photograph by M. Skiadaressis (tr); Diane L. Nordeck, Smithsonian Institution (b). **150:** From the *Codice Atlantico,* di Leonardo da Vinci, Nella Biblioteca Ambrosia di Milano, Riprodotto E. Pubblicato, dalla Regia Accademia dei Lincei, fol. 355 r,c (tl); © 1977 The Metropolitan Museum of Art, The Crosby Brown Collection of Musical Instruments, 1889 (89.4.1743) (bl); The Horniman Museum, London (c); © 1988 The Metropolitan Museum of Art, The Crosby Brown Collection of Musical Instruments, 1889 (89.4.1236) (br). **151:** INAH, CNCA,MEX; Dane Little, formerly in the collection of Valerie Franklin. **152:** Hugo Zemp (tl); Hugo Zemp (tm); Hugo Zemp (mr). **153:** Hugo Zemp (tl); Hugo Zemp (tm); Hugo Zemp (tr); Hugo Zemp (bl); Hugo Zemp (br). **154:** Hugo Zemp. **156:** Henry Eichheim Collection of Musical Instruments, Department of Music, University of

California, Santa Barbara; Courtesy of the Tokyo National Research Institute of Cultural Properties. **157:** F. Anton, Munich; Patrice Fava. **158:** Collection Musée de l'Homme, photograph by Cl. M. Delaplanche (tl); From *Greek Folk Musical Instruments,* by Fivos Anoyanakis (Athens: National Bank of Greece, 1979), pl. 35, photograph by R. Parissis (bl); Museum voor Volkenkunde, Rotterdam (br). **159:** Museum für Völkerkunde, Leipzig (tc); Timothy White, rattle made by Richard Dobson (mr). **160:** © G. Rouget (tl); Keswick Museum (tr); Collection Musée de l'Homme, photograph by Cl. M. Delaplanche (br). **161:** Hugo Zemp (tr); © 1977 The Metropolitan Museum of Art, Gift of Blumka Gallery, 1954 (54.160) (bl); From *Music: A Pictorial Archive of Woodcuts and Engravings,* selected by Jim Harter (New York: Dover Publications Inc., 1980) (lr, noisemakers). **162:** Educational Event Coordinators, San Francisco (b). **163:** Harold & Erica Van Pelt, photographers, Los Angeles (tl); Lowie Museum of Anthropology, The University of California at Berkeley (tr); Wang Mengxiang, courtesy of Pan Qixu (bl). **164:** Collection Rijksmuseum voor Volkenkunde, Leiden, Netherlands. **165:** Reproduced with permission from *Bells and Man,* by Percival Price. **166:** Deben Bhattacharya (t); The British Library (ml); Sen,oku hakko Kan (mr). **167:** From *Istoriia Kolokolov,* by Borisovich Olovianishnikov (Moscow: Izdanie T,va P.O. Olovianishnikova S,vej., 1912). **168:** From *Description of the Great Bell of Moscow,* by Auguste Comte de Montferrand, n.d., n.p. **169:** From *Description of the Great Bell of Moscow,* by Auguste Comte de Montferrand, n.d., n.p. **170:** Lydia Cabrera, *La Sociedad Secreda Abakua: Marrada Par Viejos Adeptos* (Miami: Editiones CR, 1970) (skull). **171:** Collection of The Newark Museum (11.765), Crane Collection (72.278), purchase 1972, Mathilde Oestrich Bequest Fund. **172–73:** Carol Beck and Angela Fisher. **175:** © 1990 John Werner; Mestre Acordeon Archives. **176:** Roy Boyke, *Pan Magazine,* Trinidad (t); © 1984 Bill Graham Presents Archives, photograph by Ken Friedman (bl); Martha Davis

(br). **177:** Ruta Addington. **178:** Courtesy of The New York Public Library; © 1939 RKO Radio Picture, Inc., ren. 1967 RKO General, Inc. **179:** Mary Evans Picture Library (l); © 1990 Ken Friedman (mr); From *Theorica Musicae,* by Franchinus Gaffurius (Milan: 1492) (br). **180:** John Werner (t); John Werner (mr); Steve Jennings (bl). **181:** Adger W. Cowans, © Orion Pictures Corporation, 1984 (t); John Werner (ml); Amitava Chatterjee (br). **182:** 48.461 *The Bone Player,* William Sidney Mount, American, 1807–1868, oil on canvas, 36 × 29 in. (911.4 × 73.6 cm.), bequest of Martha C. Karolik Collection of American Paintings, 1815–1865. **183:** Fred Harvey, courtesy of Museum of the American Indian, Heye Foundation (t); Courtesy of Museum of the American Indian, Heye Foundation (mr); Courtesy of Museum of the American Indian, Heye Foundation (ml); The Laura Boulton Collection, Archives of Traditional Music, Indiana University (b). **184:** Courtesy of Avedis Zildjian Co. and Lennie Dimuzio (c); Frank Driggs Collection (tr); Bob Parent (br). **185:** Courtesy of Avedis Zildjian Co. and Lennie Dimuzio (tl); William Claxton (tr); William Claxton (bl); John Werner (br). **186:** Denis J. Williams for Crescendo International; Agostino Mela, Assemini (Cagliari), Italy. **187:** Michael Ochs Archives, Venice, California; Michael Ochs Archives, Venice, California. **188:** Barbara Racy; Barbara Racy. **189:** M.,Y. Brandily, Paris, France; Barbara Racy. **190:** Hugo Zemp (bl); UNESCO—F. Pouey (bl). **191:** A.A.A. Photo, Paris, France (t); From *Exposição Etnográfica de Instrumentos Musicais e Musicais Máscaras dos Povos de Angola* (Luanda: Museu de Angola, 1964) (mr); Lowie Museum of Anthropology, The University of California at Berkeley. **192:** Schomburg Center for Research in Black Culture, The New York Public Library, Astor, Lenox, and Tilden Foundations. **193:** Eliot Elisofon, National Museum of African Art, Eliot Elisofon Archives, Smithsonian Institution (tr); Vidoc, department of the Royal

Tropical Institute, Amsterdam, Netherlands (bl). **194:** Hugo Zemp (t); Hugo Zemp (bl); © Huet,Hoa,Qui (br). **195:** P. R. Kirby, courtesy of Nan Parnell (tl); Neg. no. 330035 (photograph by Andre Cauvin), courtesy of Department of Library Services, American Museum of Natural History (c); Courtesy of the McGregor Museum, Kimberley, South Africa, from the Duggan,Cronin Collection (br). **196:** Hugo Zemp; Courtesy of Simon Mashoko. **197:** Hugo Zemp; Hugo Zemp. **198:** Alfred Gell (tl); Gerd Koch (mr); Shari Robertson (b). **199:** Courtesy of Field Museum of Natural History (neg. no. 31920), Chicago.

200: Courtesy of the President and Fellows of Harvard College, photograph by Cutler J. Coulson (tl); Courtesy of the President and Fellows of Harvard College, photograph by Cutler J. Coulson (tr); David Lewiston (ml); Larry G. Peters, Ph.D. (b). **201:** Hideo Nakajima, courtesy of Kazuo Toyoda (t); Fredric Lieberman (br); The Asia Society, New York (bl). **202:** Charles Martin, National Anthropological Archives, Smithsonian Institution; Charles Martin, National Anthropological Archives, Smithsonian Institution. **203:** Axel Poignant Archive, London (tr); Patrice Fava (bl). **204:** Michael Melford. **205:** Susumu Yoshida (mr); Michael Melford (b). **206:** Museum für Völkerkunde, Leipzig; Courtesy of Colin McPhee Collection, UCLA Ethnomusicology Archive. **207:** Courtesy of Colin McPhee Collection, UCLA Ethnomusicology Archive (t); Courtesy of Field Museum of Natural History (neg. no. 106223), Chicago (bl); Courtesy of Colin McPhee Collection, UCLA Ethnomusicology Archive (br). **208:** Hugo Zemp (t); Courtesy of Colin McPhee Collection, UCLA Ethnomusicology Archive (br); Courtesy of Field Museum of Natural History (neg. no. 35050), Chicago (bl). **209:** Scabeba Ent. Inc. (tl); David Lewiston (tc); John Werner (tr); © 1990 Carol S. Reck (b). **210:** John Werner (tr); Dilip Sinha (b). **211:** Ari Marcopoulos. **212:** Thomas Erikson; John Werner. **213:** John Werner. **217:** John Werner

INDEX

Page numbers in roman type refer to text and captions; page numbers in italic type refer to images.

Acoma Pueblo, 97, *97*
Adepoju, Sikiru, *217*
Africa, 7, 14, *14*, 15, *15*, 25, 31, *31*, 74, *83*, 84–87, 88–93, *88–93*, 138, *138*, 158, *158*, 190–96; North, *32*, *33*, 36, *36*, 87, *87*, *118–19*, 119; South, 195, *195*; West/central, 158, *158*. *See also* individual country names
Aguabella, Francisco, 177, *177*
Akan, 54, *54*
Almeida, Bira, 175, *175*
Americas, 96–99, *96*, *97*, *98*, *99*. *See also* North America; South America; individual country names
Anahata, 122
Ancestor spirits, 26, 102, 110
Angola, 191, *191*
Animal(s), 13, 14–15, *14*, *15*, 30, 50, *50*, 94–95, 150, *162–63*, *164*; soldiers, 59, *59*
Anonymous, 57, 65
Anvil, 49, 184
'Are 'Are, 77, *77*, 161, *161*, 197, *197*, 208, *208*
Armen, Jacob, 209, *209*
Armonica, 160, *160*
Ashanti, 193, *193*
Ashukhshaykhah, 130
Asia, 16, 17, 46–47, *47*, 80–82, *80*, *81*, *82*, 83, *83*, 119, *119*, 120, *120*, 122–25, *122*, *123*, *124*, *125*, 126, *127*, 128, *128*, *156*, 200–1, *203*, *204–5*. *See also* individual country names
Astarte, 33
Atumpan, 54, *54*
Aulos, 105
'Au ni mako, 197, *197*
Australia, 26, 31, *31*, 79, *79*, 154, 203, *203*
Australopithecine(s), 13, *13*
Axe, hand, 13, *13*
Aztec, 38, *38*, 39, *39*, 151, *151*

Bacchanal, 103–5, *103*, *104*, *105*
Bacchus, 103, 105, 154
Bach, Johann Sebastian, 40
Bagobo, 208, *208*
Baker, Ginger, 185, *185*
Balafon, 91, *91*
Bali, 77, *77*, 79, *79*, 121, *121*, 206, *206–7*, 208, *208*
Bamboo tube(s), struck, 197, *197*
Bamum, 159, *159*

Band, military, 56, *56*, 61
Barbados, 96, *96*
Barrel drum, 82, *82*, 87, *87*, 116, *116*, 122, *122*, 183, *183*, 190, *190*, 200, *200*, 205; mechanical, 34. *See also* individual drum names
Bass drum, 38, 74, 146, 147, *147*, 184; kettledrum, incorrectly called, 67
Bast, 33
Battle, 56, 62: of Adowa, 70, *70*; of Blenheim, 61, *61*; of the Nations, 62, *62*
Baule, 49, 51, *51*, 190, *190*, 191, *191*, 193, *193*
Beam, The, 179, *179*
Beater(s). *See* Drumstick(s)
Bell, 19, *19*, 93, *93*, 156, *162–169*; ankle, 83, *83*; anthropomorphic, 163, *163*; baby Jesus playing, 107, *107*; bowl-shaped, 157, *157*; Buddhist, 124, *125*, 156, *156*; casting, 137, 152, 166, 167, *167*; church, 162; graveyard of, 165, *165*; herder's 50, *50*; in *Hunchback of Notre Dame, The,* 178, *178*; largest, 167–69, *168*, *169*; peal of, 109, *109*; pellet, 107, *107*; ringer electrocuted; *179*, *179*; sacrifice for, 136–37, *137*; skeleton playing, 114, *114*, 115, *115; Soul of the Great Bell,* 136–37, *137. See also* individual instrument names
Belli, Remo, 147, *147*
Bellson, Louie, 184, *184*
Belt: goat-hooves, 130, *130*; sago-seed and bird-bone, 198, *198*
Ben Hur, 55, *55*
Benin, 163, *163*
Berimbau, 98, *98*, 175, *175*
Bhagavad Gita, The, 72
Bible, The, 49. *See also* specific book names
Big bang, 10–11, *11*, 211
Blacking, John, 30, 76, 99
Blades, James, 58
Blaine, Tina, 212, *212*
Blenheim Tapestry, 61, *61*
Blue Angels, noise of, 45, *45*
Blues, 40, 138, 184
Bodmer, Carl, 132, *132*
Body percussion, 13, 15, *15*, 83, *83*
Body rattle(s). *See* Rattle(s), body
Boethius, 36, *36*
Bomb, atomic, 72, *72*
Bombard(s), 166, *166*
Bonaparte, Napoleon. *See* Napoleon
Bone(s), 170, *171*; clappers, 161, *161*, 181, *181*
Bontoc Igorot, 202, *202*
Book of the Dead, Tibetan, 116
Bosch, Hieronymus, 40, *40*
Bow, musical, 31, 117, *117*. *See also* Berimbau

Brady, Matthew, 65, *65*
Brain, rhythm and the, 48
Brazil, 98, *98*, 133, *133*, 140, *140*, 141, *141*, 142, *142*, 143, *143*, 175, *175*
Bronze drum(s), 34, 162, *162–63*, 166, *166*, 206, *206*
Bruegel the Elder, Pieter, 115, *115*
Brunei, 164, *164*
Bullroarer(s), 32, 154–55; at funeral, 154, *154*; names of, 155; origin of, 26, *27*
Buriat story, 20
Burkina Faso, 52, *52*, 193, *193*
Burma, 156, *156*, 206, *206*
Bush telegraph. *See* Drum language
Bücher, Karl, 30
Bwaaanidewe'igan, 29

Cameroon, 55, *55*, 93, *93*, 159, *159*
Campbell, Joseph, 11, 17, 112, 123, 124
Canada, 74, *74*
Candomblé, 138
Cannon, 42, *42*, 165, 166, *166*
Capoeira, 98, *98*
Carnaval, 105, 140, *140*, 141, *142*, 142, *143*
Carrington, J. F., 52
Carybé, 98, *98*
Castanets, 156, 161, *161*
Caves, temple, 30, *30*
Caxixi, 175, *175*
Chad, 189, *189*
Cheyenne, 132
Children, 89, *89*, 95, *95*, 208, *208–210*, 211
China, 17, 34–35, *34–35*, 40, 67, 136–37, *137*, 184
Chopi, 195, *195*
Circle, drum, 211, 213, *213*
Clappers, 33, *33*, 84, *84*, 203, *203*; in Bacchanal, *103*, 105. *See also* Bones
Clemens, Patti, 212, *212*
Cleopatra, Queen, 48
Cliff paintings, 34, *34*
Cobham, Billy, 186, *186*
Colombia, 163, *163*
Communication, 52–54
Confucius, 7
Conga(s), 177, *177*
Constantine [Roman emperor], 105
Cook, Captain James, 135, *135*
Cortes, Hernando, 157
Cowbell(s), 184
Creation, 16–19, *16*, *17*, *19*, 107
Crotales, 32, *32*, 36, *36*
Crotals, 106, *106*, 166, *166*
Cuba, 170, *170*
Cuica, 142, *142*

Cummings, e. e., 75
Cunningham, Skip, 181, *181*
Cymbals, 73, 82, *82*, 116, 184, 206; angel playing, 106; demon playing, 84, *84*; hand, 158, *158*; in Bacchanal, *104*, 105, *105*; in monks' procession, 123, *123*; in Turkish military band, 58. *See also* Crotales
Czechoslovakia, 114, *114*

Da Vinci, Leonardo, 150, *150*
Da-daiko. See Daiko, da-
Dagomba, 89, *89*
Daiko: da-, 116, *116*; ō-, 150, *150*, 201, *201*
Damaru, 127, 171, *171*, 209, *209*. *See also* Hourglass drum
Dan, 152–53, *152–53*, 196, *196*; story, 25
Dance of the Bacchantes, 105
Dance, 30, *34*, 48, 56, 74–75, 85, *85*, 88, *88*, 90, *90*, 212, *212*; and creation, 16, 107; and rhythm, 74; and ecstasy, 77, 103; corn, 99, *99*; Dionysian, 103–104, *103*; trance, 138, *138*, *139*. *See also* Death, dance of
Dancer(s), 38, *38*, 76, 78, *78*, 80, *80*, 86, *86*, 93, *93*, 189, *189*, 193, *193*: and acrobat, 37, *37*; capoeira, 98, *98*; dervish, 100–101, *101*, *118*, 119, *119*; imperial court, 82, *82*; elephant of, 82, *82*; masked, 81, *81*, 97, *97*, 110–11, *110*, *111*; Orisha(s) and, 102, 138; skeleton, 112–16, *112*, *113*, *114*, *115*, *116*; tap, 181, *181*; with crotales, 36; with tambourine, 85, *85*
Daouli, 149, *149*
Darwin, Charles, 30
David, King, 106, *106*
D'Cuckoo, 212, *212*
Death, 62, *62*; dance of, 112–17, *112*, *113*, *114*, *115*, *116*
Defi, 149, *149*
Demolition, 45, *44–45*
Deren, Maya, 139
Dervish(es), *118*, 119, *119*; Whirling, 100–101, 101
Dewey, John, 114
Dhiplokypros, 50, *50*
Dholak, 210, *210*
Diallo, Yaya, 50, 88
Didjeridu, 31, *31*
Diegueño, 183, *183*
Ad-Din, Rashid, 55–56
Dionysus, cult of, 103
Disc(s): rattling metal, 194, *194*; whirring, 161, *161*
Dodds, Warren "Baby," 184, *184*
Dombak, 150, *150*
Donga stick(s), 91, *91*

Drake, Sir Francis, 61; drum belonging to, *61*
Drum(s), 10, 34, 35, 37, 40, 49, 55, 110, 116, 135; and bugle corps, 66, *66*; and play, 74–99; bronze, 162, *162–63*, 166, *166*; brotherhood and sisterhood of, 174; circle, 211, 213, *213*; construction of, 152, *152–53*; Drake's, 61, *61*; fife and, 56, *56*, 65, *65*, 94, *94*, 96, *96*; gourd water-, 160, *160*; -harmonica, 148, *148*; Hawaiian religious dance, 148, *148*; healing, 120, *120*; human skin, 69; hut, 53, *53*; in orchestra, 40, 42; origin of, 20, 23, 25, 29; pad, digitized, 211, *211*; penance accompanied by, 120, *120*; school, 209, *209*; talking, 52, *52*, 54, *54*; war, 56–73; "wife of the," 53. *See also* individual drum names and types
Drum-head(s). *See* Drum(s), construction of
Drum-making. *See* Drum(s), construction of
Drummer(s), 46–47, *47*, 102; angel, 41, 106, *106*, 108, *108*; boy, 65, *65*, 208, *209*, 210, *211*; clay 35, *35*; demon, 40, *40*, 41, 42, *42*; Kabuki, 201, *201*; masked, 81, *81*, 95, *95*, 110–11; master, 52, 54, *54*; mounted, *34–35*, 58, *60*;
Drumskin, world as, 211, *211*
Drumstick(s), 23, 64, 208; bone, 112, *112*; anthromorphically carved, 127; buffalo horn, 196, *196*
Duccio, Agostino di, 106, *106*
Dundun, 52, *52*

Earth: religion based on, 103; struck by meteorites, 12
Ecstasy, 77, 103, 119
Egypt, 32–33, *32*, *33*, 87, *87*, 119, *119*, 130, *130*
Ellis, Havelock, 103
England, 36, *36*, 42, *42*, 58, *58*, 61, *61*, 64, *64*, 109, *109*, 160, *160*, 186, *186*, 187, *187*
Enraged Musician, The, 42, *42*
Entrainment, 48, 70, 211; law of, 17
Ethiopia, 18, *18*, 70, *70*, 86, *86*, 91, *91*, 172–73, *173*
Europe, 94–95, *94*, *95*, 112, *112*, *113*, *114*, *115*, 116, 161, *161*, 178–79, 186–87. *See also* individual country names
Exposition, Columbian, 207

Farmer, Henry George, 64
Feld, Steven, 130
Festival(s), 78, 78; Aztec, 99, 99; Buddhist and Shinto, 205; corn dance, 99, 99; carnaval, 140, 140, 141, 142, 142, 143; Día de los Muertos [Day of the Dead], 113, 113; Hanamaki, 81, 81; of the Arts, South Pacific, 79, 79; rice-planting, 46–47, 47; Sado Okesa, 205; Shrovetide, 95, 95
Field drum, 40, 40, 59, 59, 62, 62
Field Museum, 207
Fife and drum. See Drum(s), fife and
Firdausi, Abu'l Qasim, 58
Forli, Melozzo da, 108, 108
Frame drum, 6, 33, 33, 84, 84, 87, 87, 105, 105; dervishes playing, 119, 119; women and, 32, 32, 82, 82, 103, 104, 188, 188
France, 178, 178, 179, 179
Friction drum, 95, 95, 142, 142
Funeral: bullroarer at, 154, 154; drumming at, 117, 117; human skull drum used in, 170

Gamelan, 77, 77, 206, 206–7; angklung, 208, 208
Gang-san(s), 202, 202
Garden of Earthly Delights, 40
Garrard, 66
Geiji, 166, 166
Geré, 152, 152
Germany, 31, 31, 94, 94, 112, 112, 113, 113, 114, 114, 160, 161, 165, 165, Nazi, 71, 71, 73, 73
Ghana, 54, 54, 89, 89, 193, 193
Gill, Sam, 111
Glasschord, 160, 160
God(s), 20, 25, 39, 48, 85, 110, 120, 123, 151, 151; of dance, 39, 39; of sun and rain, 47; voice of, 162
Goddess, 32, 33, 37, 110, 131; mother, 17, 18, 32, 33, 33, 103, 138
Goethe, Johann Wolfgang von, 14
Gong(s), 46–47, 47, 76, 76, 156, 208, 208; as dowry, 164, 164; helmet, 95, 95; handles, human jaw, 202, 202; in gamelan, 206, 207, 207; sound of, 162
Gorilla, 13, 15, 15
Great Spirit, 29
Greece, 50, 50, 109, 109, 149, 149, 158, 158
Grip, rudimental drummer's, 65, 65
Grosz, George, 71, 71

Grove's Dictionary of Musical Instruments, 156
Guizos, 175, 175

Haida, 74, 74
Haiti, 138, 139
Hamilton, Chico, 184, 184
Hammer(s), 49, 49
Hand clapping, 32, 86, 86
Harmonica: drum-, 148, 148; glass, 156, 160, 160; rock, 146
Hart, Mickey, 179, 179, 217
Hart, Taro, 210, 210
Hatchōgane, 80, 80
Hathor, 33
Healing. See Drum(s), healing; Rattle(s), healing; Ritual, healing
Heartbeat, 88
Hidatsa, 132, 132
Hitler, Adolf, 71, 73
Hogarth, William, 42, 42
Hohokam, 39, 39
Hokusai, 80, 80
Holbein the Younger, Hans, 112, 112, 113, 113
Holy board. See Semantron
Hopi, 38, 110, 110
Hortator(s), 55, 55
Hourglass drum, 16, 16, 52, 80, 80, 81, 81. See also individual drum names
How Universe, the Supreme Being, Makes Rain, 22, 23
Howard, Joseph, 158
Huehuetl, 39, 39, 99, 99
Human Drum, The, 68, 69
Hunchback of Notre Dame, The, (Hugo), 178, 178
Hussain, Zakir, 217
Huxley, Sir Julian, 14
Huygens, Christian, 17

Idiophone(s), 14, 30, 37, 156, 156–61, 162–70
Ilib(s), 198, 198
Inca, 69
India, 16, 16, 82, 82, 83, 83, 119, 119, 123, 123, 209, 209, 210, 210
Indonesia, 12, 12, 77, 77, 79, 79, 121, 121, 206, 206–7
Initiation ritual(s). See Percussion and initiation
Inkin, 156, 156
Instruments. See Percussion instruments
In Tubalcain's Smithy, 49, 49
Iran, 150, 150
Iraq, 32
Isis, 33
Italy, 43, 43, 105, 105, 106, 106, 150, 150, 179, 179, 186, 186
Ivory Coast, 49, 51, 51, 54, 54, 88, 88, 91, 91, 111, 111, 117, 117, 138, 138, 151, 151, 152–53, 152–53, 190, 190, 193, 193, 196, 196

Jackhammer, 44, 44
Janissary bands, Turkish, 64
Japan, 46–47, 47, 80, 80, 81, 81, 122, 122, 144–45, 145, 156, 156, 201, 201
Java, 206, 207. See also Indonesia
Jazz, 41, 138, 184
Jingling Johnny, 64, 64
John 1:1, 19
Jubal, 49
Jury, Wilhelm, 94, 94

Kabre, 31, 31
Kabuki drummers, 201, 201
Kachina, 110, 110, 111
Kaeppler, Adrienne L., 77
Kaluli, 6, 198, 198
Kamayurá Indians, 133, 133
Karagas, 125, 125
Karen people, Burmese, 206
Kauw, A., 115, 115
Kĕmpur, 207, 207
Kĕndang(s), 206, 206
Kenya, 83, 83
Kettledrums, 61, 61, 82, 82, 87, 87, 200, 200; angels playing, 18, 18, 19, 19, 106, 106; demon playing, 41, 41; in Chinese Army, 67, 67; mechanical, 150, 150; on camelback, 58, 58, 191, 191; on horseback, 60, 61, 70; skeleton playing, 113, 113
Khan, Hazrat Inayat, 193
Kin (bell), 156, 156
Kitaro, 201, 201
Ko-Ngai, 137, 137
Kodo, 144–45, 145, 204–5, 205
Korea, 81, 81, 149, 149, 200, 200
Koryak story, 23
Kotsuzumi, 80, 80
Krakatoa, 12, 12
Kromer, Martin, 49
Krupa, Gene, 184, 184
Kundu(s), 79, 79, 199, 199
Kyi-tsi, 156, 156

Laguna Pueblo, 183, 183
Langenhoeffel, Johann J. F., 105, 105
Langer, Suzanne, 30
Language, 30
Larmessin, Nicolas de, 94, 94
Laughton, Charles, 178, 178
Levi, Primo, 73
Lhendup, Dawo, 201, 201
Lieberman, Fredric, 12, 41, 202
Lightning, 8, 8–9, 18, 18, 179, 179
Likembe, 191, 191
Log(s), hollow 31, 52, 74, 74, 152, 162, 211. See also Slit-gong
Logos Seated on the Rainbow, The, 19
Lokele, 53, 53
Ludwig, William F., 63, 184

MacMurtrie, Chico, 212, 212
Make a joyful noise unto the Lord, 106
Malinke, 160, 160
Malaysia, 164, 164
Mali, 151, 151
Mandala, A., 88
Manjur, 130, 130
Maracas, 96, 96; origin of, 131. See also Rattle(s)
Mardi Gras. See Carnaval
Marimba, 206; portable, 91, 91
Mashoko, Simon, 196, 196
Mbira, 196, 196
Membrane drum. See Membranophones
Membranophones, 6, 147–51, 147, 148, 149, 150, 151
Memento mori, 112
Meteorites, 12
Mexico, 37, 37, 38, 38, 39, 39, 66, 67, 99, 99, 151, 151, 157, 157
Miango, 92, 92
Miangyo, 156, 156
Molenaer, Jan, 95, 95
Monochord, 36, 36, 179, 179
Montferrand, Auguste Ricard, 168
Moon, Keith, 187, 187
Moreira, Airto, 98, 98, 217
Morocco, 87, 87
Moropa, 195, 195
Motorin, Ivan, 167
Motorin, Mikhail, 167, 168
Mount, William Sidney, 181, 181
Mozambique, 195, 195
Mozart, Wolfgang Amadeus, 40
Mridangam, 209, 209
Mu yu, 157, 157
Mursi, 91, 91
Music: and government, 35, 40; and language, 30; origins of, 30; sacred, 40; trance, 119

Nada Brahma, 10, 17, 211
Nadel, Siegfried, 30
Nakers, 41, 41
Napoleon, 62, 62
Nature, percussive noise in, 13, 17, 38
Naubat, 82, 82
Navajo, 38
Ndengese, 90, 90
Near East, 32–33, 32, 33, 84–87, 84, 85, 86, 87, 100–101, 101, 118, 118, 119, 119, 120, 120–21, 130, 130, 188–89. See also individual country names
Nepal, 127, 127, 128, 128, 200, 200
Netherlands, 61, 61, 95, 95, 107, 107

New Britain, 199, 199
New Guinea. See Papua New Guinea
New Mexico, 38, 38
Newbolt, Sir Henry, 61
Ngo, 148
Nigeria, 83, 83, 92, 92, 163, 163, 191, 191
Noise, 10, 17, 30, 31, 40–45, 70, 113, 162, 174; industrial, 45, 212, 212; instruments of, 30, 43, 43, 161, 161, 212, 212; of cities, 42, 44–45, 44, 45; of nature, 8–9, 9, 13, 17; of war, 56, 70; rhythmically controlled, 48, 102. See also Rhythm and noise
North America, 29, 37, 37, 38, 38, 39, 39, 74, 75, 131, 131, 132, 132, 151, 151, 158, 158, 178–86. See also individual country names.

Ō-daiko. See Daiko, ō-
Oceania, 76–79, 76, 77, 78, 79, 197–99, 202
Ojibwa, 29
Oktek, 198, 198
Olatunji, Babatunde, 217
'O'o mouta, 197, 197
Oppenheimer, J. Robert, 72
Orange Free State, 195, 195
Orchestra: bronze, 206, 206–7; drum, 190, 190; gamelan, 206, 206–7; noise, 43, 43; of skeletons, 112, 113, 114; Western, 40, 42, 42
Origin of the Wooden Drum, The, 24, 25
Origins: of music, 30; of percussion, 6, 30. See also Percussion instruments: origin stories about
Orisha(s), 6, 102, 138
Owl and Eagle Lodge, 213, 213

Pacheco, Candice, 212, 212
Pad, digitized drum, 211, 211
Pahu, 148
P'ai-pan, 203, 203
Pail, five-gallon, 211, 211
Pakistan, 200, 200
Panco, José, 131, 131
Pandeiro, 140, 140, 141, 141
Pandemonium. See Noise
Pans, 176, 176
Papago, 131, 131
Papua New Guinea, 6, 78, 78, 110–11, 111, 154, 198, 199, 199; rattles in, 130
Para ni 'o'o, 208, 208
Pedasuh, 198, 198
Pedestal drum(s), 90, 90
Penis sheath, gourd, 198, 198

Percussion instruments, 144–71, *144–71;* early, 13, *13,* 30, 31–39; making of, 31, 152, *152–53;* origin stories about, 20–29, *21, 22, 24, 28,* 131, 136–37; prohibited, 106, 138. *See also* individual instrument names and types

Percussion: and initiation, 26, *110–11,* 111; and work, 49–51, *49, 50, 51;* origins of, 6, 30

Persia, 56, *56–57,* 150, *150. See also* Iran

Peru, 37, *37,* 68–69, 176, *176*

Peyote ceremony, 129, *129*

Peyote gourd, 159, *159*

Péhriska-Rúhpa, 132, *132*

Pheles, Tina, 212, *212*

Philippines, 76, *76,* 208, *208*

Picasso, Pablo, 104, *104*

Pipe band, City of Los Angeles, 180, *180*

Planet Drum, 174; Foundation, 224

Plaque, percussion, 156, *156*

Pliéwo, 151, *151*

Poland, 49, *49,* 73, *73*

Possession trance. *See* Trance, possession

Powwow drum: origins of, 29

Psalm 150, 106

Pueblo, 38

Puente, Tito, 176, *176*

Puk(s), 200, *200*

Purim, Flora, 175, *175,* 217

Pythagoras, 179, *179*

Qatar, 120, *120,* 188, *188, 189*

Quasimodo, 178, *178*

Quetzacoatl, 151, *151*

Rashaïda, 86, *86*

Ratchet, 71, 161, *161*

Rattle(s), 156, 162; ancient Egyptian, 32, *32,* 33, *33;* ankle, 92, *92,* 183, *183;* belt, goat-hooves, 130, *130;* body, 83, *83,* 130, *130;* calabash, 117, *117,* 158, *158,* 191, *191,* 196, *196;* cocoon, 83, *83,* 183, *183;* dew-claw, 132, *132;* gourd, 37, *37,* 38, *38, 39,* 97, *97,* 99, *99,* 131, 159, *159,* 193, *193;* healing, 130, *130,* 131, *131;* in New Guinea, 130; millet stalk, 158, *158;* pod, 79, *79;* raven, 158, *158–59;* shaman's, 130–33; tin-can, 83, *83,* 96, *96,* 130, *130. See also* Sistrum

Redmond, Layne, 32, 181, *181*

Religion, 17, 103

Rembrandt van Rijn, 60, *61*

Remington, Frederic, 67, *67*

Revelation 4:5, 18, *18*

Revelation of St. John the Divine, 18

Revolution, American, 62–63, *62, 63*

Rhythm, 30, 31, 174; and dance, 7; and noise, 10, 17, 30, 31, 40, 48, 102, 174; and trance, 6, 105, 119; and work, 30, 49–51, *49, 50, 51;* machines, human multidimensional, 174

Rice, planting of, *46–47, 47*

Rich, Buddy, 185, *185,* 209, *209*

Rinpoche, Khamtul, 209, *209*

Ritual, 30, 38, *110–11,* 127, 166; agricultural, *46–47, 47,* 103, 140; bronze drum in , 206; 'Cham, 116, *116;* dervish, *100–1,* 101, *118,* 119; Dionysian, 103; healing, 128, *128,* 130, *130;* initiation, *110–11,* 111; sacrificial, 34, 135, *135,* 136–37, *137;* Tawurawãnã, 133, *133*

Rnga, 200, *200*

Roach, Max, 184, *184*

Rock and roll, 40, 138

Rock Band, Richardsons' Original Monstre, 160, *160*

Rock(s): harmonica, 146, 160, *160;* resonant, 30, 31, *31*

Rouget, Gilbert, 139

Rowbatham, John Frederick, 131

Rudhyar, Dane, 38

Rudiments, European military drum, 38, 70

Rumi, Jelaluddin, 120

Russolo, Luigi, 42, 43, *43*

Rwanda, 90, *90*

Sachs, Curt, 13, 53, 85, 133

Sacrifice, 53, 152, *152;* human, 134–37, *134–35, 137. See also* Ritual, sacrificial

Salish, 74, *74*

Santería, 138

Santo Domingo Pueblo, 126

Sãnwala, 82

Saron, 77, *77*

Schaeffner, André, 125, 128, 135, 154, 160, 170

Schafer, R. Murray, 44, 49, 70, 121

Schilling, Diebold, 57

Scraper(s), 156: bone 38, *38;* metal, 117, *117*

Sculpture, percussive, 212, *212*

Seattle, Chief, 161

Semantron, 109, *109*

Senegal, 93, *93,* 121

Senufo, 88, *88,* 91, *91,* 111, *111,* 117, *117,* 194, *194;* coastal, 151, *151*

Shakespeare, William, 67

Shaman's drum, 20, 102, 125–28, *125, 126, 127, 128*

Shaman(s), 6, 20, *21,* 102, 123, 125–28, *125, 126, 127, 128,* 133, *133;* burial platform of, 128. *See also* Shamanism; Rattle(s), shaman's

Shamanism, 17, 133

Shawm, 200, *200*

Shekere, 191, *191*

Shiva, 45; Nataraja, 16, *16*

Shunko, Katsukawa, 80, *80*

Siberia, 20, 23, 125, *125,* 126, *126*

Side drum(s), 87, *87,* 180, *180*

Signal, noise and, 41

Signals, drum. *See* Rudiments, military drum

Sikkim, 124, *124,* 201, *201*

Singapore, 120, *120*

Sint Jans, Geertgen tot, 107

Sioux drum, 29

Sioux, 29

Sistrum, 33, 58, *172–73,* 173, 183, *183*

Skeleton(s), 112–16, *112, 113, 114, 115, 116*

Skull(s), 112, *112,* 116, 170, *170, 171, 171*

Slaves, 41, 91, 98, 138

Slit-drums. *See* Slit-gongs

Slit-gongs, 52, 53, 55, *55,* 77, *77,* 146, 156, 196, *196;* giant, 159, *159;* trapezoidal, 90, *90*

Snare drum, 59, *59,* 70, 96, *96,* 108, 112, *112,* 181, *181,* 184

Snare, gut, 108, *108,* 112, *112*

Solomon Islands, 77, *77,* 161, *161,* 197, *197,* 208, *208*

Sonazo, 183, *183*

Sonneborn, D. A., 116

Sotho, 195, *195*

Soul of the Great Bell, The, 136–37

South America, 37, *37,* 68, 68–69, 98, *98,* 133, *133,* 140, *140–43,* 175–77. *See also* individual country names

Spencer, Herbert, 30

Spoon(s), 87, *87*

Sri Lanka, 166, *166*

Stalactites, 30

Stamping tube, 133, *133*

Stanley, Sir Henry M., 53

Starr, Ringo, 187, *187*

Steel drum(s). *See* Pans

Sticks, concussion; 30, 31, *31;* donga, 91, *91*

Stillness, 119, 121, *122,* 122–24

Stone(s). *See* Rock(s)

Stories, 68–69. *See also* Instruments, origin stories of

Stumpf, Karl, 30

Sufi(s), *100–101,* 101, *118,* 119, *119*

Sumeria, 6

Sun, 12

Surdo, 141, *141,* 143, *143*

Surinam, 97, *97*

Surma, 91, *91*

Switzerland, 95, *95,* 115, *115*

Tabl, 85, *85,* 120, *120,* 188, *188*

Tabor, 113, *113,* 115, *115*

Tahiti, *134–35,* 135

Taiko, 116, *116, 144–5, 145,* 201, *201, 204–5,* 205

Taiwan, 157, *157,* 203, *203*

Talking drum, 52, *52,* 54, *54*

Tambour, 32. *See also* Frame drum

Tambourine, 105, 147; in Coldstream Guards band, 64, *64;* skull, 116; women playing, 32, 85, *85,* 103, 104, *104,* 181, *181. See also* Pandeiro

Taos Pueblo, 183, *183*

Tar(s), 188, *188,* 189, *189*

Tawurawãnã, 133, *133*

Temple block, 156, *156,* 157, *157*

Temple drum, antique, 149, *149*

Teniers, Abraham, 59

Tenor drum, 96, *96*

Teponaztli, 39, *39,* 99, *99,* 157, *157*

Termites, 13, *14*

Tewa, 99, *99*

Téda, 189, *189*

Thunder, 9, 13, 18

Tibet, 116, *116,* 171, *171,* 193

Timbale(s), 176, *176*

Timbila, 195, *195*

Timeline, 11–18, 30–39

Tin: box, 210, *210;* rattle, 83, *83,* 96, *96,* 130, *130*

Tinya, 176, *176*

Tlingit, 158, *158*

Togo, 31

Tom-tom, 184

Tomb figurine(s), 34, 35, *34–35*

Toolmaking, 13, *13,* 30

Tools, 10, 13, *13,* 174; sound, 30

Tortoise shell, 37, *37*

Trance, 6, 102, 105, 118–21, *118, 119, 120, 121;* possession, 6, 130, *130,* 138–39, *138, 139*

Trap set. *See* Traps

Traps, 38, 184, *184–87,* 209, *209,* 210, *210*

Treanor, John "Mambo," 180, *180*

Triangle, 106, *106*

Trinidad, 142, *142,* 176, *176*

Triumph of Death, The, 115, *115*

Tsar-Kolokol, 162, 167–69, *168, 169*

Tuchman, Barbara, 20

Tulku, Tarthang, 127, 148, 171

Tumbaga, 163, *163*

Tungda amu, 201, *201*

Tunisia, 36, *36*

Turkey, 58, *58,* 64, *64,* 84, *84, 100–101,* 101, 184

Turkish crescent. *See* Jingling Johnny

Tutsi, 90, *90*

Tuvalu, 198, *198*

Two Negro Drummers Mounted on Mules, 60, 61

United Arab Emirates, 84, *84*

United States, 44–45, *44, 45,* 62, *62,* 63, *63,* 66, *66,* 67, *67,* 72, *72,* 97, *97,* 147, *147,* 148, *148,* 178, *178, 179–85,* 209, *209, 210, 210,* 211, *211*

Universe, beginning of, 11, 17

Ur, 32

Venezuela, 133, *133*

Vibration, 10, 11

Vietnam, 202

Vili, 150, *150*

Vinayakram, T. H. "Vikku," 217

Vision of Tailfeather Woman, The, 28, 29

Voice, human, 106

Volcano, 12, *12*

Voodoo. *See* Vôdun

War, 56–73, *56–73,* 178, 202; Civil War, American, 65, *65;* Crimean, 67, *67. See also* Revolution, American

Warao, 133, *133*

Warousu, 197, *197*

Washboard, 180, *180*

Washbucket, metal, 42

Water: -drum, gourd, 160, *160,* striking, 161, *161*

Webb, Chick, 184, *184*

Webber, John, *134–35,* 135

Woodblock, 184

Wooden drum (Dan legend of) 24, *25*

Work, 30, 49–51, *49, 50, 51*

World Tree, 6, 7, 102, 127

Wrecking ball, 45, *45*

Wright, Larry, 211, *211*

Xochipilli, 39, *39*

Xylophone(s), 93, *93,* 112, *112,* 161, *161,* 194, *194:* log, 195, *195,* 206. *See also* Marimba; *Timbila*

Yakut, 128, *128*

Yaqui, 183, *183*

Zaire, 53, *53,* 90, *90,* 93, *93,* 150, *150*

Zapotec, 37, *37*

Zar, 130

ABOUT THE AUTHORS

* * * * *

Mickey Hart has been a percussionist with the Grateful Dead
for almost twenty-five years. He is the author, with Jay Stevens, of *Drumming at the Edge of Magic*
(1990). In addition, he is the executive producer of *The World* (Rykodisc),
a series of unique recordings of music from around the world. Hart has also composed
music for several television and film projects, including
Apocalypse Now, The New Twilight Zone, and *Vietnam: A Television History,* and he serves
on the board of the Smithsonian Institution's Folkways Records.
He lives in Northern California.

Fredric Lieberman, Ph.D., has taught at Brown University, the
University of Washington, and the University of California, Santa Cruz, where he is currently
professor of music and chair of the music department. He has served
as editor of the journal *Ethnomusicology* and produced field recordings and films, and
he works with Mickey Hart on *The World* recordings. He is the author of *A Chinese Zither Tutor,*
Chinese Music: An Annotated Bibliography, and numerous articles on Chinese and other
Asian musics. His current interest is American popular music.

D. A. Sonneborn is an ethnomusicologist, teacher,
award-winning composer of music for theater, dance, and film, and the author of several articles
on music and mysticism. He lives in San Anselmo, California.

* * * * *

THE PLANET DRUM FOUNDATION
of San Francisco is committed to a synthesis of people and habitat through bioregional
education. This is a step beyond conservation toward an awareness of
ecological issues based on concern for the unique natural features of local bioregions.
Visions of a positive urban future, such as *A Green
City Program for the San Francisco Bay Area & Beyond,* are among their published offerings.
For further information, write P.O. Box 31251, San Francisco, CA 94131.

A NOTE ON THE TYPE

* * * * *

Planet Drum was composed at Triad on the Macintosh.
Type families are Poliphilus, Blado, Van Dijck, and Grotesque from Monotype,
and Avenir, ITC Stone Sans, and Lithos from Adobe.